The Latest Wrinkle

and other Signs of Aging

Virginia Cornell

**Manifest
Publications**

The Latest Wrinkle
and other Signs of Aging

by Virginia Cornell

Published by: Manifest Publications
Post Office Box 429
Carpinteria, CA 930140-0429 U.S.A

Printed in United States of America

Publisher's Cataloging in Publication
(Prepared by Quality Books Inc.)

Cornell, Virginia.
    The latest wrinkle and other signs of aging / Virginia Cornell.
    p. cm.
    ISBN 0-9627896-3-1

    1. Aging—Humor—United States.   2. Aging—Psychological aspects.   I. Title.
HQ1061.C67 1996   305.26
                                      QBI96-30053

Cover design by Stewart Freshwater

Contents

Foreword is forewarned

Recently, when I realized I was careening down the road straight toward the big sign that says Six-0, I tried to swerve, slow down, stop — anything but exit. Sixty loomed, closer and closer.

I pay attention to signs, in fact I collect them. During our travels I sometimes slam on the brakes and take pictures of them — examples appear in this book. When I finally accepted there was no other route, I decided just to speed on past 60, step on the gas and head for 70. But I also decided it was time to put together some of my thoughts about aging, family and community.

Most of these essays originated in columns and articles I wrote for newspapers in the Santa Barbara area — Carpinteria Herald, Montecito Life and Goleta Sun. For eight years, I wrote a column I called "VaCuum." People often asked about the meaning of "VaCuum." For the most part, it is a play on my initials: VaC for Virginia Cornell.

One time I heard a motto that I liked: Win a few, lose a few, vacuum a few. It seemed to fit me just right. Win a few? I've had some soaring successes. Lose a few? I've had losses that hurled me into voids so dark I could not see daylight. But a person's attitude isn't formed around highs and lows. It's about vacuuming. How well do you cope with boring day-to-day messes? Take a good look at what's in the dust bag when you empty it: shards of a prized goblet you broke when you were careless, cornmeal spilled when you were in a hurry to fry fish for company, curly locks from a child's haircut. Maybe that's why it's so hard to get yourself, or anybody else, to empty a vacuum bag. We don't like to be reminded.

You can laugh or you can cry when things don't go as planned. Somewhere along the road, everybody comes to the same fork in the same road. You decide to steer toward Tragedy or Comedy. My life hasn't been any happier than anyone else's. But I'm playing the lead, so I choose to go right on laughing about spilt milk.

I would like to thank Jesse and Tisha Roth, who patiently published my weekly column for eight years. Barbara Taylor helped me choose and prepare the pieces that appear in this book. Christine Nolt, took the electronic messages from my computer discs, massaged and mixed them until Presto! They looked like a book. Stewart Freshwater, a friend and artist from Las Vegas, provided the inspiration for the cover, and then made it happen. Arlene Goldberg, Frances Laurence and Sarah Rulnick combed the galleys for goofs. Thank God for friends who are picky. Above all I thank my husband Donald Longmire, who can take a joke.

My senior year

I remember the exact moment when I gave up, and admitted to being a SENIOR. Inside, I still felt like a freckle-faced kid from Kansas. But when I looked in my mirror — the side that magnified my flaws — I didn't notice the latest freckle.

Instead, I saw the latest wrinkle.

The last time that I really wanted to be called a senior was when I was a junior in high school. At that age, who thinks of growing old? Back then, in the '50s, I don't recall that anybody referred to my grandparents as seniors. We called them old people. The term Senior Citizen was no doubt coined about the time that Del Webb staked out a bone-dry patch of desert near Phoenix and began selling Sun City. I can just see an ad executive shouting, "Find me a nice word for 'useless old codger! — with money.'" You know how euphemisms work: garbage becomes refuse; janitors become sanitary engineers; mutts become mixed-breed. Old people became Senior Citizens.

Through my 40s I tried to ignore the wrinkles that began to impress themselves on my forehead. I was too busy trying to keep my candle lit at both ends. Within a period of 10 years I earned a Ph.D., managed a ski lodge and edited my own weekly newspaper. As a single mother I saw my three children through high school and college. I even found time for some meaningful relationships. But as I neared the end of my fourth decade, the slow lane began to look mighty relaxing.

I was merely 49 years old when, in the mail, I received a letter from the American Association of Retired People inviting me to join when I turned 50. Sure, I had a few gray hairs and I had long-since resigned myself to the reality of bifocals. But I didn't think 50 was old then, and I don't think so now. I certainly was not retired. As a matter of fact, AARP's presumption made me angry. At first I refused to join.

Little by little, I began to notice that age had some advantages. About the time I turned 55, I saw that merchants were extending senior citizen discounts for theater tickets, airline travel and such. It worked this way. Maybe I was standing in line to buy a movie ticket. Maybe the ticket-seller, who had learned the hard way that people are sensitive about their age, looked over my head and shouted — as though to people behind me — any senior discounts? Maybe, through the years, I had been in the habit of fudging a little time off my age. After all, whose business was it how old I was? What a dilemma! I really wanted to save $1.50. Thrift and Vanity can be mighty quarrelsome at times.

All those things had been filtering through my mind. One memorable morning, I stopped for a cup of coffee at the McDonald's in Buellton, 50 miles north of Santa Barbara. The woman at the cash register looked at me, pointed her finger to a sign and said, "I don't mean to be rude, but please read this:"

Senior Coffee
25 Cents
60 and Older

For just a second I pondered the fact that I was merely 59. Would she demand an ID? Hardly. Nobody had bothered to "card" me since I tried to buy beer in a jazz joint in Kansas City in 1962. Besides, would anybody in the place know me? Know that I was a Senior? After only a nanosecond of hesitation I smiled at her calmly and said, "One senior coffee, please."

I was naughty! I lied about my age. On the other hand, I've stuffed so many Big Macs and Quarter Pounders into children and grandchildren that I earned that 25-cent cup of coffee. And I wasn't going to stand in that line for six months waiting until it was legal to get it.

But suddenly, I found myself confronted with a lot of questions. Am I required to act my age? Should I donate my blue jeans to charity? Should I shelve my ambitions to keep writing books? And when, exactly, does a senior become a senior? Social Security won't consider me a senior for two more years when I reach 62. I'd better stay healthy, because Medicare won't take care of me until I'm 65.

A lot of advertising, for everything from computers to designer jeans, brags about bringing you "The Latest Wrinkle." Why should I be any different, even though "The Latest Wrinkle" just appeared on my cheek? In my heart, I'm still that freckled-face kid from Kansas.

Good gifts come in tall packages

Occasionally a lonely widow or divorcee asks how I managed to find a husband. After sixteen years of divorced, single motherhood, the last thing I ever expected was to be married again. So I tell them a Christmas story, but it is also a love story.

It was nearly Christmas of 1983 when I sat in my little house in Tabernash, Colorado, addressing cards. For the previous few years I hadn't sent any. Christmas is the busiest season in a ski area. Caring for the hordes of visitors who arrive, intent on enjoying a white Christmas, leaves little time for festive chores.

But in September of that year I had sold my newspaper business. At long last I had a little time to myself. Because it had been neglected for several years, my address book was a shabby mess of scratched-out street numbers, business cards and odd scraps of paper. Would my cards reach their destinations? People move around so much.

I paused to wonder where I would be the next year at Christmas time. I really hadn't a clue. My children were grown; I no longer wanted to live in the mountains. Winters were long and so harsh it was impossible to take out the garbage without donning a parka and snow boots. Very soon I would be looking for a different place to live and possibly a change of career.

To celebrate my new freedom, I decided to treat

myself to a winter vacation. I wanted to put my feet down in a place where nobody even owned snow boots. California would be nice. I figured I could drive my car to San Francisco then work my way south to San Diego, visiting friends along the way. Visions of ocean waves danced in my head.

In a note at the bottom of some cards, I warned my California friends they might expect me in February. I wrote to a couple I had been close to for more than 20 years. Off went their card, addressed to Carpinteria.

By return mail, I received a reply. It was from the male half of the Carpinteria couple. It said, "My wife left three and a half years ago. But please come see me."

I thought, why not? Little did I realize my life was about to change — drastically, and for the better. I had never thought of Don Longmire as a potential husband, but suddenly the idea made sense. He was the proverbial tall, dark and handsome guy. Besides, there were water pipes running along the foundation on the outside of his house. That meant those pipes would never freeze!

A visit of a few days led to a longer stay. Before long, I was persuaded to move here. In late August of 1984 I married the man who replied to the Christmas card. And I can truly say we have lived happily ever after.

My advice is, pay attention to your Christmas card list. By all means, seek out the whereabouts of friends from years past. Death or divorce can cause pain and loneliness. A suddenly single person often thinks, "I wonder what ever happened to that nice friend? We always had fun together." Christmas cards are a subtle way to check up on things like that.

So don't neglect to keep your Christmas card list updated. It could be the start of something big!

Sex among the blossoms

May is the month when the sweet scent of cherimoya blossoms wafts through the orchard. The enticing aroma beckons us to administer to the sexual needs of the exotic fruits. Nobody has written a song about this romantic custom, but they will. They will.

I'm still astounded by how few people, many of them right here in the Santa Barbara area, have ever experienced the incredible taste of these tropical delights. The flavor is a little like pineapple, a little like a banana, a little like a pear only much, much better than any of those. The skin is light green, thin and the fruit looks as though someone pressed thumb prints all over it; the meat is pale yellow and can be scooped out with a spoon. Hard black seeds are easily disposed of.

The fruit remains expensive. Harvested from December through April, the "cream of the crop" is immediately flown to Japan where people are willing to pay outlandish sums to sample its delicate flavor. People from Latin America, Asia and Africa are also familiar with cherimoyas. Much of the rest of the crop is snatched up in the ethnic markets of Southern California.

Cherimoya is a difficult name to remember. For the record, it rhymes with 'chair annoy ya.' I can't tell you how depressed I was when a friend rushed up to me after a luncheon and said, "I just loved your Chernobyl."

Trust me, the cherimoya is the fruit of the future.

When my husband, in an annual ceremony, brings in the first cherimoya blossom of the season, I know that soon we will devote our cocktail hour to the sexual needs of the cherimoya. Typical tropical lovers, they become amorous every afternoon.

In many ways, cherimoyas do things backwards. Spring is when the trees' old leaves turn from green to yellow to brown and drop off. Simultaneously, the branches sprout tiny new leaves. Funny trees, June signals the ebb of their attractiveness; they look as dowdy as molting birds or lizards.

About the same time, they begin to bloom. That's where I come in because cherimoyas need help with pollination. I'm not sure what kind of insect gets the job done in Chile and other Latin American countries where the local trees come from, but no indigenous bug has become hooked on cherimoya nectar. A few get pollinated naturally, but the yield won't be very satisfactory unless we take an active hand in the breeding process.

One reason bees may be reluctant to take on the chore is because the blossoms are tough to find. Cherimoya leaves are green. Cherimoya fruit are green. Cherimoya blossoms are green — it's green, green, green down in the grove. (The song is getting clearer.) If I take a glass of wine with me, to cheer me while I pollinate throughout the cocktail hour, I must be sure it is red wine. A glass of white wine gets lost amid the green.

We pollinate our small stand of cherimoyas the old-fashioned way. We use a Kodak film can because they are black; I can see the stamens against the side of the can. We locate a "giver" blossom, or a very mature one, from which the pollen can be easily scraped or shaken out. With the help of a tiny artist's brush, we collect pollen in the can.

Then we look for female, or "receiver" blossoms. Actually, the blossoms seem to be girls early in the afternoon and boys later, as they bulge in the heat. I can usually tell a receiver because the blossom is tighter. I don't want to give away any female secrets, but I look for ones with their legs crossed. Dipping the brush into the pollen, I shove it up her blossom! If I'm doing the job properly, blossoms are giggling down in the grove. Once you get past the embarrassment of what you're doing, it's fun.

My husband was born to work with trees because he is very tall. I wish I could wear stilts during pollination, so I could encourage more fruit to "set" higher up. Sometimes an individual fruit will weigh five pounds, so it would be nice if it started out life higher in the tree.

I like pollination time. It is very pleasant to have an excuse to take a glass of wine out to the orchard, to move about among the fragrant trees and to just enjoy the warm afternoons of summer.

But, "I'll be with you in cherimoya blossom time" lacks universal appeal.

The Delia conspiracy

Because I had been a bride once before, I knew that if I wanted to change anything about my husband I'd better get on the project fast. There's a window of opportunity open to brides that will likely bang shut after the first few breezes. I pounced on the chance to reform one or two bad habits Don had fallen into during his prolonged spell of bachelorhood.

Lacking a human dinner companion, he and his beautiful eleven-year-old Doberman sat down each evening to dinner. The sleek, shiny animal sat at attention next to his chair, her big brown eyes fixed on his every move. Long ribbons of drool flowed down from her jowls. The only way to stanch them was to slip something into her mouth so her saliva had something to work on. Maybe Zuti (short for Zutana, a variety of avocado) wasn't everybody's idea of a gracious dinner companion but she was always available. One of the reasons I fell in love with Don was because of the gentle way he treated his dog and two cats.

While I didn't kid myself that I was any more beautiful than the pedigreed Zuti, I know I was a better conversationalist. I learned to love animals from my mother, but she had a firm rule against feeding pets from the table. Woe unto anybody who attempted to sneak a treat from their dinner to the dog. So I laid down the law in my house, too. No treats from the table! Don pleaded that Zuti's old heart would be broken, but I held firm.

Reluctantly, my husband agreed not to feed her. The dog learned pretty quickly that the good times were over, so she gave up and slept in the corner while we ate.

When you marry into a family, you not only get instant pets — you get instant in-laws. My parents had been dead for several years, but my 60-year-old groom's mother was over 90. Delia was a lovely woman, tall, frail. She lived in an assisted-care situation near one of Don's sisters. One day, his sister brought Delia to visit us. Although I had cooked thousands of breakfasts in my life, I went to considerable pains to be sure this one was one of the best. It's difficult to be casual, the first time you cook for your mother-in-law.

Upon arriving, Delia hugged her son then greeted Zuti and the cats. How sad for her there were no pets where she lived. The animals may or may not have remembered her, but they recognized an animal lover at once. The cats rubbed her ankles and the dog presented herself to be petted.

When we sat down to eat, I saw an astonishing thing. Zuti pushed right by me, sat by Delia's side and started salivating. No question about it. She remembered Grandma!

Delia took a substantial helping of everything. I was pleased that she seemed hungry and liked my cooking. To my astonishment, Delia put one bite of food on her fork and into her mouth, then with her fingers she pinched eggs from her plate, passed her arm clear over her body, and tucked the bite into the dog's mouth.

Zuti looked at me as if to say, "You could learn a thing or two from this lady. She knows how to do things right!"

For every bite of food Delia took, the dog got one, too.

My husband looked at me, a little uncomfortable about his mother's behavior, but I motioned him not to worry about it. I wasn't about to confront with his 92-year-old mother about her table manners.

In the years since our marriage my husband and our pets have conspired in an ongoing attempt to change my rules. If I have been out of town for a few days, I notice the animals are circling the table in eager anticipation at mealtime. I pride myself that I have always been able to train animals. Husbands are much more difficult.

Taming his inner brat

My beloved is a curmudgeon. The dictionary defines curmudgeon as irascible and miserly, often an old man. A curmudgeon is sometimes confused with a crank, but in my experience a true curmudgeon thinks of himself merely as loyal to the opinions he has seasoned for a lifetime. I don't think of my partner as old, but irascible and miserly fit well enough.

I was still a bride when I first realized I had a curmudgeon on my hands. I was appalled. By all accounts, he would probably be difficult to deal with. But with maturity comes the realization that any Prince Charming is bound to arrive with a wart or two.

The dictionary isn't sure where the term curmudgeon comes from — extensive research has not determined whether its origins are Old English, Latin or "other." But I'm one up on the lexicographers because I know that curmudgeon must be a back-formation from a lost verb: *mudge*. What is to *mudge*? A *mudge* is to complain, to direct an unsolicited comment toward a target that can't possibly reply. What curmudgeons had to *mudge* about before TV was invented, I can't imagine.

Don hates beards. "Can't trust him! He has a beard!" Never mind that the guy on TV is a Nobel scientist or eminent physician. If he has a beard, his information is suspect.

He's dubious of weathermen, too. Californians are as

picky about weather as they are about wine. If the day isn't perfect, they want to dial an 800 number and send it back. I try to explain that weathermen like Willard Scott often act silly so they can serve as foils or clowns to serious anchorpeople, just to lighten up the news hour. He doesn't care, he loathes their attempts at humor.

At first, I tried to reason with Don when he loudly proclaimed, "I know how to solve this problem. Shoot them!" That solution covered a multitude of heinous sins. Perhaps I'm more liberal because I preached tolerance, understanding. I invited him to walk a mile in the other person's moccasins. "Why would I want to do that?" he countered.

Fortunately, after only a few months of marriage I realized that my husband's daily mental health depends on a couple of good mudges first thing in the morning. Either he releases a string of invectives against his latest peeve or he carries around his anger, bottled up like a can of warm beer, all day. It's better if he pops sooner rather than later.

Set in his ways? You bet. Yet my curmudgeon has no trouble at all getting in touch with what is popularly known as his "inner child." One day, as we strolled through a parking lot, Don disappeared. When I looked around he was underneath one of those monster trucks with wheels big enough to hold up a Boeing 747. He was inspecting its suspension. trying to figure out gear ratios and such. I was apprehensive. What if some teenage thug with attitude came roaring up yelling, "What you doin' messin' with my truck?"

My husband will never have any trouble getting in touch with his inner child. The biggest problem is how he will keep his inner brat under control.

He piled the woodpile higher

Hello, I'm C.D. Miller and I wrote a book!" A short
man with a shiny bald head thrust forth his paw
toward a startled fellow who was leveling his Winnebago
in a campground. The scene was repeated over and over
throughout Father's travels. I wish I could have been a tree
squirrel so I could have seen the surprise that greeted his
proclamation. How many campers have ever met the author
of a book? He usually made a sale.

Father wrote a book, printed 2,000 copies of it, then
peddled it through the campgrounds of the West. He didn't
start writing it until 1972, when he was 72 years old. He
called it: *Leave the Woodpile Higher Than You Found It.*
Into it went his life's philosophy — essays on everything
from marriage to school discipline to the English language.
But maybe I should quote from the first few pages:

Let us enter this book through the North
Woods. The musical syncopation accompanying the
sounds of the woods is the thud, thud of my axe,
beloved tool very close to me as long as I can
remember. Spasmodically this low, dull sound is
interrupted by the shrill, creaking stridulation of
splitting wood, fire wood.

One July morning, 1933, my wife, Trudy, and
our sons Dwight and Elwood unpacked our folding
boat, duffle, and provisions for a journey up the
Tahquamenon River, some 30 miles west of Sault

Ste. Marie, Michigan, coastal of Lake Superior. This 11-foot craft, powered by a single cylinder tiny "kicker" had bourne us along the Mississippi brakes, over the Manistee in Michigan, and afloat the risky waters between St. Ignace and Mackinac Island.

Dwight was a redheaded tyke aged six. Elwood was eight. They loved to swim, make sandpiles, fish, set up the tent — and fight. Hard times. I was in Kansas Education then, a superintendent. We had no money. But we had all summer. And we had the woods, wild cherries, fish, blueberries, flour. Above all, we had each other.

Throughout the picturesque Tahquamenon there were families of waterfowl paddling along the plashy brinks; and here and there a deer thrust its curious head through wreaths of undergrowth to regard us as we floated by. When the afternoon began to wear late, we became uneasy about a place to dock. Suddenly, we came upon a tiny cabin, and a cleared area. A sign made us welcome. Rule of the woods was that backcountry cabins are never locked, but were built for the convenience of hardy and earnest venturers.

Outside the cabin, under the overhang of the roof was a carefully stacked rick of split wood, dry, brittle, tinctured with gum terpentine. Very quickly the campfire was roaring, sending up the familiar pleasant pine odor. When the fire had subsided, the glowing coals were ready for that camp cooking whose pervading aroma stirred and tantalized utterly our sensory systems, for we were ravenously hungry.

Now just above the woodpile was a lettered sign, whittled into a slab of rough board. What do you suppose those letters spelled out?

Friend, Leave This Woodpile Higher Than You Found It.

Of course, the next morning my father busied himself with splitting a stack of wood. That sign became my father's credo — and not a bad one at that.

Some psychologists believe that our lives are "scripted." If so, I was destined to write a book called *Doc Susie,* perhaps because my father left the woodpile higher than he found it and willed that I should, too. Then I published it and sold copies a few at a time — but not in campgrounds. More important, I keep measuring my own accomplishments in life against that woodpile.

How mama came out in the wash

My mother was a dignified woman, a Sunday School teacher, an exemplary parent and as my father never tired of saying, "A most remarkable woman." Fortunately, she didn't take any of her splendid virtues very seriously. How well I remember the day when Mama rode the bucking Bendix.

Our house in Wichita had four stories; it was a grand old home, built in 1902 on a street called Park Place. But unlike the street on the Monopoly board, ours was no longer in a fashionable area of town. My dad paid $3,500 for it in 1941 and it took him three whole years to pay for it!

My dad had several hobbies and prided himself on keeping up with the latest technology. His up-to-date gas furnace stood in the center of the basement, surrounded by his darkroom, wood working shop, projectors for his slide and movie shows. Mother's area was smaller. It contained her pantry, deep freeze, ironing board, a washing machine and even a mangle — to iron the sheets, of course. When was the last time you slept on an ironed sheet?

My father indulged several expensive hobbies, but he always took pride in furnishing Mother with the latest household gadget. If he was satisfied that Mother was well equipped, he suffered less guilt when he bought himself a new camera. So when Bendix marketed the first front-loading, automatic washing machines, Papa declared that our old wringer model was history. Mother was perfectly happy with her agitator, wringer and tubs. But she didn't hold out against him for long.

My father wrestled the machine down the basement stairs, uncrated it, hastily bolted it to the floor and proclaimed it ready for use. Keep in mind that those first automatic washers spun the clothes with roughly the same amount of force it requires to lift off a helicopter. The machine really did make Mondays a lot easier, and a "Bendix Stop" was on the tour when Dad showed guests around the house.

One day, while I was struggling over my hated algebra, I heard a terrible scream come up the stairs from the basement. I also heard a clattering and banging as I hurled myself down the steps, two at a time, to see a very strange sight. My normally staid mother was spread-eagled across the top of the washing machine, which was hopping across the basement floor. It was bucking, trying to toss her off.

"The plug," she screamed, "Pull the plug."

I did, and the mighty machine halted in its tracks.

My mother buried her face in her arm, her plump body seemed still to be heaving in rhythm with the leaping machine. Great sobbing sounds came from her throat.

I was truly frightened. "Mother, Mother. Are you all right?"

"I will be," she lifted her chin, "as soon as I . . . can stop laughing." She reached behind her bifocals to wipe tears from her eyes.

What I had mistaken for sobs was a series of explosive chortles, "That must have been the funniest sight in Sedgwick County," she said. "I'm so glad you got to see it. Now maybe Clifford will bolt this thing down properly."

She explained that she thought she could hold down the machine while she reached over it to pull the plug, but the machine got away. It was a frightening event; most women would have gone into hysterics. But Mom and I sat on the basement steps, hugging and laughing.

When father came home he was aghast, of course, "You could have been badly hurt." He pulled a long face. Father's face could be very long indeed because he was bald and there was so much of it. He hastened to the lumber yard to buy a bag of concrete. He not only bolted, but cemented the machine in place.

That night at dinner, he couldn't understand why my mother and I kept breaking into giggles and wiping our eyes.

My mother was a bit discouraged when I paid little attention to her tips on cooking and cleaning. But she imparted a skill that has been more valuable to me than either of those. She taught me how to laugh at myself. Lots of people never get the knack of it.

Todo — we're in Kansas all right

We blew into in Kansas, which advertises itself as the Land of Aaahs, in my brother Woodie's mammoth motor home. It lacked the velocity of Dorothy's twister, but was more dependable. My brothers and I were headed for our Webster-Wells family reunion. I didn't know it, but soon I would see ghosts.

At the first of the many rest stops that line I-70 across Kansas, we braved the prairie wind and gusted toward restrooms. Then, on a whim, we sailed through an open door that announced the Kansas Tourist Bureau. Across a crowded room a loud twang reverberated: "Welcome to Kansas, have a cup of coffee." We looked over rows and rows of brochure racks to see a friendly lady, who was pushing maps. It was tough trying to choose between the Fick Fossil Museum in Oakley, the Dalton Gang Hideout (and tunnel) in Meade or the World's Largest Hand Dug Well. That's in Greensburg, the town where I was born. There was also a School Teacher's Hall of Fame somewhere. It was a shame we had to pass up the World's Largest Ball of String as we hurried on our way. Heck, some attractions weren't even advertised. In one little town, the twin water towers were painted: Hot and Cold.

My brother, who intended to impress his relatives with his motor home, soon discovered that everybody else was thinking big, too. A wagon train of elaborate rigs was already circled, protectively, in front of our host's home when we arrived.

At first I despaired of seeing anybody I recognized. That branch of my family had been enthusiastically engaged in a feud during most of my formative years. Consequently, I met first cousins from the other side of the fray — relatives whose names I had only heard. Besides, cousins I had played hide-and-seek with had suddenly become grandparents and I had trouble figuring out who they were.

The future population of Kansas is assured. There were little kids everywhere! They were crawling up the driveway, suspended from canvas swings, staring out from plastic shells, eating gravel, emerging from beneath picnic tables.

When the wind finally died down and a firefly or two came out to cheer the evening, strange things began to appear.

I rubbed my eyes when I saw my Uncle Pete sitting there eating cake! He was an auctioneer who used to cry sales all over Western Kansas, selling more beef than Wendy's in his time. But Uncle Pete had been dead for five years.

No, the genial fellow sitting there wasn't Uncle Pete, it was his son, my cousin Jerry. I hadn't seen Jerry for a long, long time and the stringy kid who raised 4-H sheep had assumed the shape of his father.

I caught my breath when I saw my beloved mother across the room. That comfortable, witty lady who fed me, tended me and made me behave was over there dishing up potato salad. If I could just get over there fast enough, she would hug me again . . .

But she turned out to be my Aunt Margie. Since I had

last seen her, the soft waves atop her head had turned to silver. Now she looked just like Trudy, my mother who had been dead for a decade.

Could it be, that we were becoming our elders?

The reunion lasted just one night, long enough to visit, find ghosts and wonder at the diversity in our shared gene pool. Time to be genial, not enough time to fan fires of the feud.

Kansas truly was the Land of Aaahs.

When animals sniff and tell

We named our next dog Jammer so we could have a set: The Cats and Jammer. One night all three seemed to sense that we were running away to join the circus, that they would be left at home. Those little sideways glances — you know how a small animal can whip guilt on big humans. Our brown dog Jammer looked particularly miserable as she sat gazing out the window, ignoring me. She always does that when she senses she is about to be abandoned.

My husband and I weren't even taking grandchildren with us! We don't need an excuse to indulge in something we both love. Every couple of years, a circus called Carson and Barnes pitches a huge tent on the Carpinteria Bluffs. As we strolled along the dusty parking lot we were like two little kids, anticipating the myriad smells of popcorn, dust, straw and exotic animals.

Above the hot dogs and peanuts wafted the exotic odor of elephants and big cats. As we stood looking at a particularly handsome tiger, then glancing at the bottom of his cage, my husband said: "Jammer would surely be interested in this."

Like all dogs, our Jammer is into scatology. When we take walks here on the side of Shepard Mesa, she makes it her business to investigate each little lump. And sometimes she seems to tell me what she's found:

"Hey, a raccoon was through here about an hour ago."

Sniff. Sniff. "Hmmm. Bobcat. Haven't smelled that for a while."

"Just another neutered dog. No big deal."

But the scent that really sends the hair bristling on her neck is coyote. A mere sniff sets her dashing across the hillside, and occasionally she even flushes one of her wild cousins out of the lemon grove. Scat, scat, scat. She lives for it.

I believe that a big light bulb lit up above our heads simultaneously. If we couldn't take the Cats and Jammer to the circus, why not take the circus to them? Or at least the part that would interest them most.

Those circus folks must've seen everything in their day. The tiger man was talking to a girl. When my husband interrupted: "Could I have a little of your animal's left-behinds?" he didn't flicker an eyelid. But he did warn us not to try to use what he was about to give us in our compost heap. Too strong.

Then we found the elephant man. He obliged us by using his shovel to scoop a sample into another plastic bag. My husband locked our dubious treasure in the car, and we proceeded to enjoy the trapeze artists, the jugglers, the clowns and all the circus acts — immensely.

Afterwards, we drove home beneath a beautiful, half moon. With the windows rolled down. We could hardly wait to test our animals' reactions.

We decided to reveal our surprise a little at a time. First, we let the cats out of the house. Our gray cat, Frizz, took a sniff and looked at us with that, "Are you crazy?" look that cats occasionally muster, and quickly went back in the house.

Old Waylon walked away in disgust — with a slight

twitch of what would be a tail on any cat but a Manx.

Then we released Jammer. I think she smelled something powerfully strange the moment she ran out the front door. She raced to the car, sniffed all around the trunk lid, and nearly went berserk when Don let her sniff one corner of the plastic bag. Her hair stood two inches atop the scruff of her neck and she chased madly up and down the driveway. She seemed to shout, "Good Lord! What went through here a few minutes ago? Did you see anything? It must've been big, really big!"

Do our pets ever realize what lengths we will go to in an effort to keep them entertained?

Jammer would hardly wait until the next morning so she could tell Otis and Sam and Zeke, and her other doggy friends. "Guess what my folks brought home from the circus? Would you like to smell my souvenir?"

Lots of grafts on this family tree

One of my grandsons, a bright lad of nine named Ian, cast his big blue eyes in my direction and asked, "How can I figure out my family tree?" Fair enough, grandparents are put on this earth for the purpose of answering questions. After all for so many years I've had all of the answers but my own children rarely asked.

While he and his half-brother, Daniel, watched, I got out a piece of paper, started limbing out little bars for him to fill in with the names of grandfathers, great-grandmothers, aunts and uncles.

All went well until he asked, "And where do I put your name?" This child is no blood relation whatsoever to me. He calls me "Grandma," but in fact he is the son of the woman who married my stepson. Dear reader, are you confused? Well if you are, think how the kid must feel. Except through Adam and Eve, it's going to be tough to establish a relationship. So I suggested to the boys that on such a lovely afternoon they ought to go out and enjoy the swing in the eucalyptus tree while I pondered.

Ian calls a whole passel of people by the name Grandpa or Grandma. Maybe as many as eight. Not one of his grandparents is still married to the person he or she started out with. Some are biologically eligible for the "family tree," but others are step in-laws like me.

Years ago, this child and I agreed that when people asked if he was my grandson, we'd just say "yes" to avoid complicated explanations. Actually, there are eight cute little kids who call me grandma; not one of them is "blood relation." I long ago decided that being a family means that love and respect rank above claiming the same DNA.

Come to think of it, maybe there's a reason why so many of my peers are "into" genealogy these days. One of my friends takes an adult education course in how to research her ancestors. Another travels all over the world hunting up progenitors. But face it, this ultimate decade of the 20th century may be the last crack anybody will ever have at making sense of family trees.

But back to the kid. If he's confused about his divorced and remarried grandparents, it's going to get a whole lot worse. People aren't at all shy these days about revealing how their children entered the family through the means of adoption, single parenthood, artificial insemination, test tubes, even surrogate motherhood. Situations that used to be whispered about are now announced within five minutes of being introduced to a new acquaintance.

Family trees are constantly grafted, pruned, cross-pollinated and thinned. The family tree of the future will look less like a tree and more like creeping ivy.

I can just see the day when this child is showing his own grandchildren the family album. "Your Uncle Ralph used to tell us jokes. He was a real clone. All of his duplicates told the same stories."

It's the docent thing to do

The child was about 11 years old. He was slightly taller than the other sixth graders I was leading through the Santa Barbara Museum of Art. Although it was clear his straight black hair had been combed when his mother sent him to school that morning, cowlicks escaped at roguish angles. His brown, round Mexican-American eyes seemed to suck the paintings right off the wall. He had never seen anything like these works by Chagall and Monet.

But his nose was bleeding.

I spoke to an adult, a mother who accompanied his group, "Perhaps you should take him to the restroom."

"No, no," the boy protested.

"He doesn't want to miss anything," the woman said.

Fortunately, I had stuffed a wad of clean tissues into my pocket before I left the house that morning. I didn't want to embarrass the kid, so I slipped him fresh Kleenex and tried to act as though bleeding was included in any art museum tour. In 10 minutes or so, he was all right.

For some reason, that kid's nosebleed reminds me how important my volunteer efforts at the museum really are. Each week, when I arrive at the museum to give a tour, I try to remember that most of the children who come have never been in any kind of museum, let alone an art museum. I hope they will remember the museum as a friendly place, and want to return. And maybe, just maybe, a child whose exposure to culture has been limited to television will realize that there are more important things in life — and aspire to them.

Sometimes I hear a retired person say, "I raised four kids, now it's my turn."

Or, "I worked for a living and paid taxes. I put in my time." These are their excuses for failing to volunteer in the community.

While I won't quibble that their lives were well lived, is there nothing that they feel so passionately about that they want to share it with the next generation? Have they never been touched by personal tragedy to the extent that they want to get involved with a crusade or raise money for a cause? Have they no obsessions? Do they feel no obligation to return a little something to the land that has been generous?

I really admire people who are obsessed.

Years ago when I lived in Phoenix, we sometimes enjoyed a day's outing along back roads on the desert. When we came to a crossroads, we frequently saw a crude sign with letters painted in black across the lid of a paint can. It might say 13.5 N 8 W. That meant that we were thirteen and a half miles north and eight miles west of the intersection of Central and VanBuren, the crossroads of downtown Phoenix. They were put there by a housepainter named Denny Gleason who didn't want anybody to get lost — an especially hazardous peril during hot Arizona summers. So he had conceived his own system for marking telephone poles and fenceposts. The signs were everywhere. He must have been a very successful painter, to have so many lids. And he must have spent all of his spare time mapping where they were to go, painting them and putting them up.

When I first moved to California, I met a woman who had decided that young people could be helped if they would just learn to stand up straight. She was convinced that the world could be saved through good posture. At schools and Girls Clubs she made presentations, teaching young people how to carry themselves with grace and dignity. "It's about self-esteem," she said. Why not? You've got to start someplace.

As for me, I really believe that children need to know about art, literature and music. In an age when taxpayers are urging "back to basics," it's probably up to me and the other people who feel the same way to expose children to the ultimate fruits of civilization. I always think back to my father's book — *Leave the Woodpile Higher Than You Found It.*

And I think about the kid who liked art so much he wouldn't pay attention to his bloody nose.

A rose by any other name is harder to spell

My maiden name, birth name, original name, the name on my birth certificate, was Miller. People who are born with a name like Miller may be the last people to get interested in genealogy. Where do you start? Consequently, it is interesting to live with somebody who has an unusual name.

You know if your name is unusual. If your name is Johnson, Smith, Garcia or Brown wrong numbers are about the only unpredictable thing that happens when the phone rings. But if your name is peculiar, each phone call can be an adventure. Two or three times a year the telephone rings at our house with somebody at the other end claiming to have the same name as my husband — Longmire. When I call him to the phone he has a jolly chat, citing people with the same last name who live all the way from Los Angeles to Oregon to the English Lake Country to Germany to the Isle of Man.

When we travel, my husband always looks himself up in the phone book. For example, he said there were seven listings of his name in the Manhattan phone book. Fortunately, the hotel charged for phone calls so he didn't bother to ring them up.

But a name like Miller is a big yawn. I can't recall that anybody ever came up to me to ask: Are you any relation to Arthur? or to Marilyn, Mitch, Ann, Glenn — or even Dusty — for that matter. Look up Miller in the Manhattan phone book? Are you kidding? The question is not how many Millers are in the book but how many columns of Millers are in it.

The downside of having an unusual name is that nobody seems able to spell it right. Although my husband carefully spells his name out loud, we get lots of mail addressed to Longmeier, Longmyer, Longwire, Lungemire, even Lungmire.

Perhaps my attitude explains why I clung to Cornell, even after my first marriage crashed and burned. I thought it sounded like it belonged on a writer. Besides, I sort of enjoyed it when people asked: "Like the University? Like Katherine?"

Surprise yourself on your birthday!

When I see a red poppy bobbling along, atop a wide-brimmed straw hat, I know that beneath it is Barbara Taylor. She is taking her daily walk along the streets of our home town, Carpinteria. Everybody waves at the familiar lady who is blonde, quick to smile. She walks, purposefully, with a cane. Most days she marches four miles with the same determination she once applied to helping others in her career as a registered nurse. But now she devotes her medical knowledge to her private battle against a tenacious enemy: rheumatoid arthritis.

Her goal is to keep moving, to keep her joints in action. I've admired her determination since we first met, as fellow docents at the Santa Barbara Museum of Art. One day over lunch we discovered our mutual passion for football. She grew up in Massillon, Ohio. Massillon is to football what Boston is to beans, what Hershey is to chocolate. When she was in high school, Paul Brown — who went on to found the Cleveland Browns — was the coach. Massillon is also where she was raised with a strict code of Mennonite values. She learned to be modest, never to call attention to herself. It was there that she trained for one of the few careers accepted for women in the 1930's — registered nurse.

Although she kicked over more than her share of traces between leaving Massillon and settling in Carpinteria, she still felt a strange itch. The only problem was, she wasn't quite sure just where to scratch.

Events of her seventy-fourth year will be all too familiar to other arthritis sufferers. She underwent separate surgeries to replace a knee and an ankle joint. There was nothing special about that — except that First Lieutenant Barbara's new joints were courtesy of the Veteran's Administration. Along with other women who served in World War II, she had to struggle to get the Veteran's Administration to recognize that our country owed servicewomen the same medical care it routinely offered men. The women's orthopedic ward at the VA hospital in Los Angeles consists of just one room.

Perhaps Barbara's service experiences in Europe left her with permanent travel hunger because what little money Barbara can hoard from Social Security, she spends on travel. Somehow, between knee and ankle surgeries, she managed a tour of Spain. It was during a side trip to Tangier that something big, something important, something wonderful happened. In a cabaret, she saw a belly dancer.

She resolved to learn the art — just as soon as she got her ankle retooled. Still on crutches, she enrolled herself in a belly dancing class. Never mind that her ankle was still in a cast. There was nothing wrong with her belly. Nobody calls it "ankle dancing."

In class, she stood in place and learned to "shake it." As soon as she got her cast off, she added footwork. As her birthday approached she made herself a costume, she recorded the music. Eight very special friends (all that would fit in her tiny apartment) didn't know what a big surprise was awaiting them. The place was redolent with the smells of the delicious Moroccan food she had concocted for the occasion.

After everybody had a relaxing glass of wine, she excused herself to her bedroom, donned extra veils, turned on a tape recorder then burst into her living room — fingers chiming bells, belly shaking. Sixteen eyes wept with amusement and admiration as Barbara whirled around the tiny room like a dervish, peeling off veils as she rotated her pelvis.

When it was all over, Barbara was very pleased with herself. The next day she told me, "All my life I wanted to do something wild like this. And if I can't do it on my 75th Birthday, when am I going to do it?"

Why not give a surprise party on your birthday? You can surprise everybody else!

She dressed her grandchildren in white

When I opened up my silverware chest, shiny metal beamed into my eyes with the intensity of an arc welder. The sterling was a gift from my first husband's mother. I hadn't thought about her for a long, long time.

Nothing ever worked out quite right for Edna; her husband just owned a good-old-boy gas station in Shawnee, Kansas; she was just a clerk at the A&P market in nearby Mission. She could have put up with those indignities if her only child had followed a career she planned for him: either brain surgery or the concert stage. He was just a school teacher. I was young, and didn't understand that the illusions were all that remained of the grandiose dreams she treasured as a young woman. She frequently hinted that when we weren't around she was a social butterfly who moved in the best society in Mission Hills, the exclusive Kansas City suburb. She frequently dropped the names of people I had never heard of.

All too soon after her son and I were married, we presented her with three grandchildren. I thought that most of her ideas about how to raise children were mighty peculiar, especially the part where she liked to dress them all in white outfits to take them to the zoo.

One day, she offered me a set of silverware she had been accumulating for several years. Allsweet margarine had an offer on its package. Purchasers could save coupons, send them in with a little cash and collect a set of sterling silver. You'd better believe it was a long-running offer. Their distributor made Edna a deal: for every 100 cases of Allsweet margarine she rang up at her register at the A&P, his company would give her one piece of flatware. She faithfully kept track of every pound she rang up.

I was not as impressed with the gift as I should have been. I'm ashamed to admit that the only reason I accepted it was because it was sterling. Before she retired, I had a complete set for 12, clear down to the iced tea spoons and fish forks. But I thought to myself that someday I might try to trade the silver for a pattern more to my liking. I guess I had a few pretensions of my own.

The years flew by. My husband and I were divorced after 11 years of turmoil. A couple of winters later, Edna died after an agonizing struggle against bone cancer. I managed to raise my children, and since they were normal, independent kids they weren't perfect either. Not one of them became a brain surgeon or a concert pianist.

I even became a mother-in-law myself.

That day, when I opened the silverware chest, the enormity of her gift finally impressed me. I counted the number of pieces. How many cases of margarine was that? And how many times did her tired fingers hit the cash register so that I might have something nice? I remembered how gnarled and sore her toes always looked after standing on concrete floors all day. I was so impatient with the woman, probably judgmental and rude as well. Still, I wouldn't wish to have her back. I doubt that I would like her any better just because I'm older and wiser.

But I wish I could tell Edna that nobody could get me to trade that silverware for anything.

God makes them cute —
so you don't kill them

Do you remember your worst moment as a parent? The occasion when everything went wrong, all at once?

Mine was one morning in 1961 when my first husband was finishing up his master's degree in education at the University of Kansas. I had given birth to my third, and youngest child 10 days earlier, so I was still sore. Her brothers weren't much older. July in Kansas, without air conditioning, is a special kind of hell all its own. But in just four more days we would have to give up our student apartment because we were moving to Phoenix. It might as well have been Rangoon, it seemed so far away.

No move is easy. I'd rather be dragged along the ground behind a runaway horse than to move, even in the best of circumstances. This was the worst of circumstances. Half-filled cartons yawned throughout our trash-strewn rooms. I needed to sort and pack for five people. We had no idea where we would live when we got to Arizona.

Some people think that taking care of a newborn baby is a challenge. It's tougher when you have two active toddlers, aged one and a half and two and a half. To complicate matters, their father suffered from an impacted wisdom tooth. He had retired to the couch with an ice bag, blurred his consciousness with pain pills and declared himself incapable of doing one darned thing. As I recall, he was reading Michener's *Hawaii* to keep his mind off his problems. My mother had been with me for a few days, but left because she wanted to be with my father on their wedding anniversary.

No wonder I had a migraine headache. If you suffer from them, I don't have to tell you how the tiniest shaft of sunlight pierces your eyeballs like a sword; how if you even turn over in bed, nausea empties the contents of your stomach; how your skull just isn't big enough to hold your brain which pulses stronger than your heart.

After I fed my baby daughter, I fell back into bed with her asleep at my side. I was barely conscious when, from another room, I heard the ominous sound of little children giggling, shouting with glee. Next to screams of pain, no noise alarms a mother more than prolonged giggles. Children don't sound like that when they are playing in an approved manner.

I staggered to the kitchen, clutching Drew like a football on one hip, one hand pressed to my forehead. Something crunched beneath my bare feet. I had difficulty focusing my sore eyes because they could barely believe what they beheld.

Two naked little boys had spread Cheerios all over the top of our seafoam green formica table. Keith, the oldest added a few corn flakes for texture, then spilled some milk. Gordon was slathering the mess around, like he would in their sand pile. Then the boys climbed up onto the table and were surfing back and forth on their little bellies, using milk as a lubricant. They paused occasionally to fling cereal at each other, like confetti.

Around the kitchen, none too tidy in the first place, milk droplets coursed down cabinet fronts. The mess —

which was rapidly turning from crunchy to soggy — oozed over the top of the table onto the vinyl padded chrome chairs and cascaded down onto the linoleum. The boys were so pleased with themselves, so happy. They were transcendent with joy and their puckish faces grinned like characters right out of a Norman Rockwell magazine cover. They were surprised, possibly disappointed, that I didn't share in their joy.

No judge who had ever been a parent would have convicted me if I had killed them. Fortunately, I knew that if I were to touch either of them, I probably would have.

From then on, I had a base line from which to judge domestic mayhem. Was it as bad as that morning in 1961, back in Kansas?

Clean out your closet before someone else dies!

Ghosts are dwelling in my closet. Sometimes I'm afraid to slide the door open for fear that the empty sleeve of a jacket I haven't worn for three years will bend its elbow and point at me in accusation: "Get rid of me, get rid of me like it says in that article about cleaning out your closets." I'd like to get rid of it and a lot else — but I need an exorcist before I can do it.

A couple of times a year, usually when the seasons change, I resolve to clean my closets. I steel myself for the chore of tossing out last year's fashion statements. Then I resolve to phase out waist bands that will no longer stretch the distance around my middle. As I sort, stack the clothing that I intend to donate to the thrift store. "Poor people at the thrift shop don't care if these are last year's trend." But an increasing number of items refuse to follow their fellow castoffs into the big plastic bag of oblivion.

How can I part with the beige wool sweater — the one I must protect every year to prevent silverfish and moths from devouring it? I rarely wear wool where I live in California. The sweater is heavy, it's too hot and it itches; the yarn has sort of bunched up so it doesn't fit very well. I don't think it has been on my shoulders for four or five years.

But my mother knitted that sweater and she'll never knit another.

A tattered old towel on the shelf is starting to ravel at its edges; the color has faded from orange to pink. It isn't worth anything except as a rag. But as I rub it across my cheek I remember how I got it.

It was a cold afternoon in Denver. My friend Claire, who had been my buddy for 16 years, decided that my shabby bathroom needed a drastic overhaul. I don't like shopping much, but Claire dragged me to a mall. She promised she would paint my bathroom if I would buy new towels and a shower curtain. If there's anything I hate worse than shopping it's painting, so together we chose coral towels, a bright shower curtain printed with sea birds and a big fuzzy rug. When she painted the bathroom a pale peach color and we draped it with new linen, it looked warm and wonderful.

But Claire was killed a few years later in a car-train accident. We won't shop together again.

Unfortunately, I was invited to help myself to some of her clothes. Never mind that Claire was six feet tall — she towered seven inches above me. I did take a few things. Big mistake! I can't part with her blouses although they bag to my knees.

I seem to be a careless person because each year I lose more friends. They may go, but their contributions to my closet remain. It's getting so I hate to accept gifts or hand-me-downs.

What they don't tell you in those magazine articles is to hurry so you can get rid of things from your closet before whoever gave them to you dies! I know that some veterans groups pass on a bottle of whiskey; the last survivor gets to drink it. I'm afraid that if I live a long life I may find myself marooned, the last survivor in a closet full of clothes!

Degree of gratitude

Graduation time is when prestigous schools, which spend most of the year pleading for the government to give them grants because they are serious research universities, hand out honorary degrees to celebrities like Merle Haggard. Maybe they hope that newspapers and TV will give publicity to the ceremonies at good old I.O.U.

Meanwhile, outgoing seniors take advantage of the occasion to protest against the government that made this momentous event possible. Understandably, taxpayers are outraged. Just about the only people taking things seriously are the parents — who have bought every sneaker, pencil and lunch ticket that it took to get the kid out of school. Parents are the ones who are dressed up, in contrast to the graduates who sport cut-offs beneath their academic gowns.

At a high school graduation we assume that the proudest parents must be those of the class valedictorian. Hah! The happiest parents are the ones who thought there was never a prayer that their kid would make it through. If you look around, you will see they are the ones crying buckets of joy.

I've been there. Maybe you have a kid like my son Gordon — there are many more Gordons than valedictorians. Gordon treated high school with all the seriousness he would a buffet line in a restaurant. He liked to taste courses before he committed himself to a full helping. If he didn't like the way algebra tasted, he'd try business math instead. If he couldn't digest that, he tried to leave it on his plate and hope nobody would make him finish it. For all those reasons, his transcript was something of a hash. It was all that we could do to sandwich enough courses together to cook up a major so he could graduate.

As I sat in the auditorium on that June day I was watching the gym teacher out of the corner of my eye with some apprehension. Only three days before he had sent a nasty-gram home with Gordon to inform me that my son's chances of graduating were severely diminished by the fact that he had not reported a clean gym suit for two months. What was I supposed to do at that point? Wash it extra times? I just knew he was going to blow his whistle, grab my kid by his mortar board, defrock him and hurl him back into the junior class.

When I see one of those bumper stickers on a car saying: "My son earned academic honors at Local High" I feel a pang of envy. If I had ever been presented with one of those things I probably would have pasted it across my forehead.

But in the long run things turned out OK. I'm happy to say there is life after barely graduating. Gordon knocked around for a few years, then enrolled himself in a university and struggled through it. School was never easy for him, but eventually he took it seriously.

Sometimes fate is kind. By a fluke of fate, his high school gym teacher happened to be in the audience. He actually saw Gordon get a diploma from a four-year university. For just a second I wished I still had that gym suit so I could rub his nose in it.

Love — it just is

People are always welcome at the studio of Beatrice Wood, the world famous 103-year-old potter who lives near Ojai. The day I visited she was perched on a bench, talking to a group of admirers who sat on the floor, their necks craned as they gazed up to her in awe. Swathed in a dramatic sari, adorned by ethnic jewelry, she spoke in the dramatic tones she cultivated in her youth, when she studied to become an actress.

When Beatrice Wood talks — people listen. After all, how many people live to see 100, let alone continue to produce lusterware bowls that sell to art museums for five figures?

Candid, occasionally outrageous in her opinions, she was clearly relishing the occasion. "I leave the business to someone else, so I can sit here and talk to young men. I hate being the boss. It takes away my silliness and I need it." Perhaps, yet everyone in the room is aware that she is an excellent business woman who has marketed herself well. She swears that her advanced age can be attributed to "Chocolate and young men."

"Beato," is how she signs her pieces and is known to her friends. But Beatrice Wood's enormous creativity began when she started shaping her own life. At age 14 she announced that she was going off to live the bohemian life. After a series of dreadful scenes, her mother allowed her to go to Paris where she studied drawing.

When she returned to New York she became acquainted with Marcel Duchamp, whose cubist painting "Nude Descending a Staircase" scandalized the public at the 1913 Armory Show. An artistic and intimate relationship followed, during which she produced some pictures so erotically suggestive that when they were displayed at a show, gentlemen left their calling cards!

She neither denies nor affirms the rumor that her relationship with Duchamp and Henri Pierre Roche served as the model for the latter's novel, Jules and Jim. Later, Francois Truffaut made it into a movie. When the Dada group in New York broke up, Wood followed her collector friends — Walter and Louise Arensberg — who had moved to California. About that same time, she became interested in the Theosophist movement and its leader Krishnamurti.

Beatrice Wood came to pottery in a way that will be familiar to many seniors: she took an adult education class at Hollywood High School. She had bought several luster-glazed plates in Holland, but could not find a teapot to match. She decided to take a class and make one. She expected that within 24 hours she could approximate their finish. The glaze she applied to her first teapot didn't satisfy her; consequently, she kept right on doing pots for the next 60 years. She claims that many of her startlingly beautiful glazes result by accident: "I'm the battered wife of that kiln."

Her strong, graceful fingers gesture an emphasis to her opinions. The vibrant intelligence that informs every syllable renders her ageless. "I don't try to work every day," she says. "I do work every day."

Although her bowls, glazed with such sheen that it is difficult to believe they are not metal, are her principal claim to fame, she abandons herself from time to time to the pleasure of creating witty figurative sculptures — tiny little people, often engaged in suggestive interplay. The figurative pieces don't sell as well, but provide an outlet for her spontaneity and wit. She claims to enjoy making both types equally.

She hasn't escaped the effects of age. In her nineties, Beatrice became quite deaf. "If I had to lose one of my senses, hearing is the one I can most easily do without," she says.

Someone at her feet shouted, asking if she had any children, any family. Without hesitation she replied: "I have three children — and they all have tails," referring to her yellow dog Rajah and her two cats. "The other day I sat on my couch. My two cats were beside me and I stroked one and then the other. I said, Oh kitty, I love you so much. But I love you, too. Now which of you do I love the most?'

"I debated and debated. Then suddenly it came to me. Love cannot be measured. It just is."

How to rescue a gray hound

My dog Jammer started turning gray around her chops when she was merely seven years old. Let's see, if one human year equals seven dog years. . . Yipes! Forty-nine! No wonder she started turning gray. Oh sure, my hair is getting gray, too. Fortunately, the only time I have to fret about my own grizzled locks is when I look in a mirror. We don't have many in our house; I haven't bought a mirror since I was thirty-five.

But I can't help looking at Jammer. My canine companion is 75 pounds of brown dog. When I got her as a tiny puppy at the County Pound, they told me she was probably a mix of weimaraner, doberman and rhodesian ridgeback. She is slim, muscular and elegant. If it weren't for her gray chin, you could never guess her age.

I like to think of myself as remaining aloof from the silliness some people lavish on their pets. I wretch when I see a picture of a poodle wearing an Easter bonnet or a yellow labrador sporting sunglasses. Of course my dog is different. OK, OK I'm probably guilty of being a bit foolish when it comes to my hound. After all, she's better behaved than my kids ever were — and more attentive, too. She begs for food, but never money. She has yet to call me in the middle of the night after wrecking my car.

Just when I start believing that my sweet, exceptional, wonderful dog has climbed one rung higher on the evolutionary ladder than other people's dogs — Jammer reminds me of her canine ancestry by doing something totally disgusting.

From time to time I watch in horror as she snatches some small rodent from the grass and swallows it whole! Occasionally she grabs a snack from the compost heap. One day she paraded around the yard with a stalk of celery dangling from her lip — like Groucho Marx with a cigar. It seemed to me that she winked as she wiggled it.

When I brought home a bag of steer manure to apply to the lawn, my dog took one sniff and marked it with — you know. She looked genuinely distressed when she saw me dispersing the fertilizer on the lawn. She seemed to say: "You're not going to throw away this perfectly good stuff are you? What a waste!" To prove my folly she fell to her knees and rolled in it — her tongue hanging out through a gloriously happy dog grin.

Unfortunately, that's not the worst thing she ever rolled in.

Jammer is a country dog, but I'll bet the fanciest poodle at the Westminster Dog Show would react the same way. Given their bestial behavior, there must be a human quirk that makes us want to do silly things for our dogs — indulgences we wouldn't even allow ourselves. So I got to thinking. If there were a preparation I could smear on Jammer's muzzle to conceal the gray — something nontoxic — she would look half her age.

Is there a doggy beauty formula called Grecian Muzzle?

Women are pack animals

Any small child can tell you the difference between a mommy and a daddy.

A mommy carries a purse.

I remember my very first purse. It came from Woolworths, was pink plastic and it had a little zipper inside for my coins. My mother urged me to save my allowance and "put it in my purse." Of course I lost it on the bus with my $3.32 in it and never saw it again, despite the fact that I had filled out the I.D. card. I had such faith someone would read my I.D. card and phone to report finding my purse..

In high school, girls carried "clutches," teeny purses designed to carry just a small wallet plus a lipstick. Then came my first driver's license. My first credit card. My first calendar. Eventually, there came a time when I didn't carry a purse. No, I carried a diaper bag instead. Somewhere between the prom and the pram I picked up a heavy luggage habit.

Taking inventory and cleaning out a purse can be more sobering than a Methodist picnic. There's a paperback book I started reading three months ago. A perfume sample I picked up but don't like. A travel alarm clock that needs a new battery but I keep forgetting to buy one. A calculator, just in case I need it, but I never seem to.

Any woman walking down the street is really a traveling litter bag. We wouldn't dream of defacing the environment so the recesses of our purses are jammed with candy bar wrappers, receipts, flattened Coke cans, ruined Kleenex, flyers for pizza parlors and busted balloons. Women who are fanatics about emptying the kitchen wastebasket daily will clean a purse only twice a year.

I've often heard men say, with an air of superiority, "I don't know why you are toting that thing around. All I need is a wallet, pocket comb and a handkerchief."

Sure. But when he needs a Tum for his tummy or a pencil or a piece of paper to write on, where does he turn? And when he fears that the small package he has just acquired will ruin his sartorial profile if he shoves it into a pocket, who does he ask to carry it? These refrains are frequently heard: "Honey, do you have any Tic Tacs in your purse? I don't suppose you have any chewing gum? Do you have a pen and paper? Stick this brochure in your bag."

I've tried many alternatives. I've stuck everything into a backpack, only to find myself struggling in and out of the straps every time I need change. I've carried an executive briefcase, which in a few weeks became so heavy with my normal purse items that I couldn't open it in public for fear that my face powder would settle a fine dust on a committee meeting. I bought a vest, but I bulged like a mule fitted out to pack into the Sierras.

I've pondered this phenomenon a bit lately, and I think I finally have it figured out. The rise of purses fits in roughly with the demise of woman as a nomadic animal. When women were no longer required to pull their tepees and beef jerky from campsite to campsite on a travois, some man invented the purse.

Then he invented the notion that carrying one isn't a manly thing to do.

Wiping away the evidence

We were invited to a Christmas luncheon at a beautiful home on the Riviera, an exclusive area in Santa Barbara. Most of the 80 people in attendance were women, fellow docents from the art museum.

I will not tell you how the house was filled with silver candlesticks towering over banks of poinsettias. I will not describe the elegant buffet, nor the scrumptious specialty dishes provided by our members. Nor will I describe the luncheon conversation, which was stimulating, elevated, cultured.

Out of the 80, I was at least number 65 to visit the facilities — located in a little powder room off the foyer. When I washed my hands you can imagine my amazement when I saw tiny, pristine linen guest towels hanging on the bar. They were so neatly pressed that any fool could see they had not been used!

Had the 64 refined, well-educated guests who preceded me neglected to wash their hands?

Unlikely.

Had each and every one of them dried their fingers on toilet paper, then flushed away the evidence to avoid mussing up the towels?

Likely.

What a situation!

I knew that our hostess had dedicated herself to perfecting her gracious home. She shopped for antiques, read all the magazines, knew what was right and then proceeded to do things that way. A regular little Martha Stewart, she was. Would she think she had invited a bunch of Neanderthals to her party if nobody used those towels?

Well, you can guess what I did. I grabbed two of them and dried my hands ostentatiously; I mussed them and made them look violated so the next person wouldn't mind using them, too. A strange thing happened as I twisted the linen around my fingers. A wonderful feeling of power and freedom rushed through my temples. What had I done? I felt positively naughty, as though I had violated social taboos and lived to tell of it.

That night I got to pondering.

Obviously, there are two mighty forces at work when it comes to the subject of guest towels. First, there was Mother. My mother often said: "Don't use the guest towels. We're saving them for good. Dry your hands on a bath towel."

Many moons later bath towels and face cloths belonging to a set had been washed over and over until they were limp. But the fat, lazy guest towels just draped smugly over their towel bars, retaining their dye while their working friends got paler and thinner.

The second great force at work? Mother, again. A little later on, my mother tried to reverse herself and explained that guest towels are provided so company would have something dainty and clean to use. So when one is a guest, it is all right to dry fingers on them.

What's a kid to do? I knew for sure that I had been pounced on for using one of those guest towels that was "saved for good," so I wasn't about to take any chances — especially in someone else's house! Our generation of guests secretly reaches beneath the bath towel and dries our hands on the back of it. We conceal all evidence that would link us to personal hygiene.

Secret finger drying works unless, as happened to the ladies at the luncheon, there is no bath towel available.

But just when I decided to damn the torpedoes and use guest towels — another hostess vexed me by providing pretty little paper towels for her guests. Let's see. If there are six paper towels spread out like a fan on the bathroom counter and there are 25 guests, if I use one will there be enough for everybody?

MOTHER!

Obit bites back

When my son Gordon was a third grader, he started reading the *Phoenix Gazette*. The blonde, curly headed kid would ask me to explain stock reports, sports box scores, TV schedules. He figured out the comics for himself.

One day when he was reading the paper he discovered the obituaries and asked me about them. I explained that when someone died the newspaper ran a notice so people would know about the funeral. Often, a reporter wrote something nice about that person's life. Gordon started reading obituaries to me, aloud. Did I know Franklin Brown, Harriet Livingston, Graciela Garcia? He was always disappointed when I said no, but read me the obit anyhow — clear through next-of-kin. After a few days, when it didn't seem to him that I knew anybody in Phoenix, he made what he thought was a reasonable request: "Hey Mom, give me the names of some of your friends and I'll tell you if they died."

Later, when I owned a rural weekly newspaper, we used to run lengthy obituaries when local cowboys or merchants died. Alan Best, my managing editor, liked to write them. To him, small fish mattered as much as big fish in our tiny pond. When a quiet old Indian everybody called "Chief" died, Alan wrote: "Chief always lifted his long-necked beer bottle by the label to drink from it. He said it kept the beer colder." It's nice to be remembered for something.

When the town drunk died we published some of his favorite sayings including: "Just because a pancake is flat don't mean it doesn't have two sides to it."

I made a problem for myself when Sam, the ratty old town dog who had been hanging around the pizza pub begging for pepperoni for years, keeled over. I published a tender farewell, recalling the time he got busted by the police. When the pharmacist locked up for the day, he didn't know that he stranded Sam in his drug store. When he became frantic to get out, the dog set off the burglar alarm. It made so much noise that everybody in town ran to the store to see what was the matter. People were looking through the plate glass door, laughing, while Sam contented himself with eating candy bars. He didn't mind when it took a long time for the Sheriff to hunt up the pharmacist so he could unlock the door. Readers thought the piece was funny.

But from then on, every time someone's pet died its owner wanted an obit in the paper. Hey, when your best advertiser, in tears, calls to say her poodle died, you're not going to turn down a request for a eulogy.

These days when a person dies, newspapers often charge the next of kin for printing a few nice words about the deceased. I don't approve of this practice. But I can sympathize with the newspaper. It's difficult to know where to draw the line.

A friend of mine, Anne Johnson, sometimes teaches creative writing classes for seniors. She invites her students to compose their own obituaries. Her exercise is intended to focus writers on what has been important in their lives. "Besides," she says, "if you don't do it, God knows what your kids will say about you!"

The ultimate cruise

During the holidays my husband and I faced the annual problem of what to get each other for Christmas. A cruise? A new stereo? An easy-to-program VCR? Our wants are simple; somewhere in the recent past we became the man and woman who have everything, or at least everything we really want.

One day early in December the love of my life asked, "Shall we join the Neptune Society together?" Silly me, I figured he had been talking to our travel agent.

"Will it get us a better deal on a cruise?"

"No, it's a cremation plan. Pay now and when the time comes they scatter your ashes at sea or else send them to our kids. Whichever we want."

At first I was a little shocked. "That's more like walking the plank together," I commented. "Is that really what you want for Christmas?"

He gave me grin and nodded in the negative.

Even though it made me a tad squeamish to think about it, I knew it was the sensible thing to do. My own parents left very precise instructions about how they wanted their remains to be handled; when they died, it made things a lot easier for my brothers and me.

My husband made the arrangements, but I was not looking forward to the appointment. One morning this Neptune Society sales guy arrived at our house in a black Porsche — such an appropriate color. He was an earnest yuppie type, wearing a sports shirt, tie, blue jeans and, so help me God, black and white cowhide loafers.

Like most of the people I've met who make their living in the funeral industry, he was a jolly guy. When he explained the whole process he made it sound as easy as shipping something FedEx. "Pick you up, stick you in a box, off to the crematorium, scatter you at sea while somebody reads the Lord's Prayer."

Elegantly simple. Hey, they ought to market their services through the L.L. Bean catalog. Or maybe some year it would make the ultimate "His and Hers" Neiman Marcus Christmas gift if they throw in a jeweled urn.

The young man asked us how we would like to pay for our exit visa, so to speak. "You can pay cash, we'll finance it or you can put it on your credit card. Do you have one of those cards that gives you frequent flier miles? You can charge it and get mileage credit." The guy was positively ingenious.

When you think about it, planning for the future — all of it — is a romantic thing to do. But on the whole, I'd prefer a cruise to Bermuda.

His and Hers tourist attractions

My husband said, "I don't wanna go to Butchart Gardens."

His protest didn't surprise me particularly. Long ago he decided that any public attraction that advertises itself on billboards must be "just like Disneyland." Not that he's ever been to Disneyland. He justifies his prejudice by explaining that he dislikes crowds and distrusts mechanical contrivances. Consequently, I've had to drag him kicking and screaming to attractions he did like when he got there — such as Monterey Bay Aquarium and Colonial Williamsburg.

"Why don't you want to go to Butchart Gardens?"

"I've been there. With my folks."

With his folks? They hadn't traveled together since Pearl Harbor!

I stood firm. "Sorry dear. You'll just have to indulge me because I want to go. After all, how often do I get to Victoria, B.C.?"

The gardens were as plotted, tended and flamboyant as a small army of uniformed gardeners could make them. It's true that there were a lot of tourists — most of them speaking Chinese and German. Interesting thing about language: "Wow!" translates as pretty, universally. I was impressed by the dozens of eager gardeners whose sole job description seemed to be lopping rose blossoms.

As we circled the Fountain of the Three Sturgeons,

passed through the Rose Garden and headed toward the Sunken Garden, I was annoyed by a raucous noise. The brochure mentioned that the Sunken Garden was once a limestone quarry, but we weren't expecting to see bulldozers and dump trucks in action. As we drew closer, it sounded as though somebody was trying to blaze a superhighway through the hydrangeas.

But I quickly forgot the commotion when I saw Ross Fountain. After the lifetime I've spent battling frozen pipes and leaky valves, I'm awestruck by any piece of plumbing that works consistently and predictably. Dancing waters? They're a miracle.

So far, my husband had been on his good behavior. I could tell he wasn't as impressed with that fountain in the grotto as I was. I sat down on a bench to watch the waters wave, waft, spiral, spray, shoot and bubble. I quickly forgot the obnoxious racket coming from behind the trees. After a few fidgets my husband said, "I'll be right back." I figured he wanted to find the men's room.

After fifteen minutes or so he returned, a big happy grin on his face. His long arms flailed gestures of glee, "They've got the biggest wrecking ball I ever saw over there. Thump, thud! They're tearing down an old factory or something."

"How'd you get in there?"

"Oh, I asked one of the park guards to let me see what was going on. He took me through a gate and told some of the workmen I was his uncle."

You want the perfect tourist attraction? One with universal appeal for him and her? How about signs along the road that say, "See the World's Most Beautiful Garden and Largest Wrecking Ball."

Jonathan Peach Pit

In July, we ate a peach that grew on a tree in our orchard. There's nothing remarkable in that, you may say. In July many families eat peaches they grow themselves. This is the story of a special peach.

A few years ago a little boy named Jonathan, our grandson, was visiting his father in Goleta. In a situation that is all too common these days, he spent 11 months with his mother in Phoenix and one month with his father in California.

One day Jonathan ate a peach and said, "I'll plant the seed."

"It won't grow," warned his father.

"They never sprout," said his stepmother.

"Oh yes it will," Jonathan said with the faith a five-year-old brings to any project. The towheaded kid stuck the pit in the ground next to the patio. The following spring his stepmother was surprised and pleased when it sprouted. On his next visit Jonathan tasted the joy that comes with those wonderful words, "I told you so."

Jonathan loved to hear people talking about his tree, which grew very fast. "You're a regular Johnny Peach Pit," I teased. I don't think he had any idea what I meant. On each visit, Jonathan checked the tree's progress; its vigorous growth made him happy.

When he was eight, Jonathan was killed in a terrible accident. While his Phoenix family was moving to a new house, a truck loaded with furniture ran over him.

Of course, the peach tree became a symbolic treasure. But its very existence was threatened by another situation that was all too common these days. His California family, facing the threat of unemployment, decided to move to Colorado.

One of their first concerns was what to do about the three-foot tree. So in February, after the last leaf fell off the tree, his father dug it up then replanted it here, at his own father's house in Carpinteria, in hopes it would survive. The family gathered around the tree and blessed it.

All spring we watched that tree with anticipation. We were relieved when leaves started to form, jubilant when the tree bloomed. Eventually we counted nine little peaches. Jonathan's grandfather was vigilant in protecting the tender tree from the ravenous gophers that chew along our hillside in search of tender roots.

I've never seen a tree produce so much fruit in such a short time. Maybe it knew how precious time would be. I made a little jar of jam from the peaches and sent it to his family in Colorado. How can a peach taste sweet and sad at the same time?

Sometimes a great notion

When the I Magnin store closed in Santa Barbara I was sad, but not really surprised. All department stores are a dying breed. I know what killed them.

When I was growing up in Wichita, it was a big thrill when my mother would say, "I need some thread and snaps, let's go to downtown." We got dressed up and rode the bus. Alighting at Douglas and Broadway, mother headed straight for the notion's department at a store named Bucks. She and a knowledgeable sales lady would discuss zippers, and decide which one would be right for the dress mother was making. If the notions department at Bucks didn't have what she needed, we would proceed to an even grander store called Innes.

While we were at it, we always checked out the adjacent fabric department. Mother loved to look at yard goods, paw through pattern books. I never learned to sew, despite my mother's valiant attempts to teach me. But I still like to hang around bolts of fabric — to feel their flat silkiness, to smell their new sizing. I love the pleasant flop, flop noise a bolt makes when it is flipped over and over while the clerk measures out the yardage.

The hat department was right on our path to notions. Mother loved hats, could not resist trying them on. Once in a while she broke down and bought one. She was always a little embarrassed, a little giggly when she took it home to show my father. Because my mother was a thrifty soul —

who always bought for the rest of the family first — my father was always pleased when she indulged herself.

But I doubt mother would have gone to town or spent money on herself at all — had she not had the excuse of needing something from "notions." Her quest for shoe trees or knitting needles drew her into a store more frequently than advertising.

Once there, she frequently bought something else on impulse. On rare occasions, she even took me to lunch in the store's tea room where I put little rosettes of butter on hot clover-leaf rolls. Heaven.

Sometime in the 1960's, some guy fresh out of business school got the bright idea to analyze sales — department by department. I can just see this man looking over his sales sheets. "This notions department is nickel and dime stuff. Don't make any money on it. Labor intensive. Get rid of it."

Would the same guy, analyzing sales of a hardware store, say, "Screws don't make any money. Quit stocking them."

It didn't take my mom very long to figure out that if she couldn't find what she needed in notions there was no point going into the store. So she didn't buy her cloth there, either. Naturally, the fabric department was the next to be eliminated.

All too soon, a worse disaster followed. The lady in ready-to-wear who smelled nice and said, "May I help you?" disappeared. Remember her? When you said you wanted a blue dress she started pulling hangers off racks, lugging garments to your dressing room, offering an opinion when asked. In her place, a worried looking person stood next to the cash register, poring over computer printouts. Her new responsibility was to continuously count and check off the whereabouts of merchandise.

Instead of "May I help you?" the refrain became, "If you've found what you want, I'll take time out from doing something important to ring it up."

What killed department stores? Merchandising experts. That's what.

My money is where my mouth is

Attention Baby Boomers. Invest now in the ultimate status symbol — one that will make you the envy of your peers well into the 21st Century. But you won't find it in the Neiman Marcus catalog. Instead, look in your dentist's office.

One day I pulled into the parking lot at my periodontist's office. There, in its pristine glory, sat a beautiful Silver Cloud Rolls Royce; I mused to myself that perhaps life is fair after all. Bad gums afflict the rich as well as the middle class.

As I entered the waiting room, there was no question about who had driven her Roller to the dentist. Gracefully seated on the couch was an older woman, beautifully dressed and coiffed in a manner which can be achieved by anybody who has unlimited funds in carefully diversified holdings. Diamonds sparkled from here and there about her tasteful person. It was difficult to figure out how old she was. As we both reached for the same magazine, we fell into conversation — the way strangers will in an airplane or a waiting room. I said something about dreading the impending deep cleaning. She took it upon herself to correct my attitude.

"I have a most amusing story to tell you. A few weeks ago I was in the hospital for a little surgery." It didn't sound like it was going to be amusing.

"The nurse put a cup in front of my nose and said,

'Put your teeth in here.' She left the room and came back and demanded: 'Well, where are your teeth?' "She couldn't believe it when I told her my teeth were my own and I wasn't giving them to anyone!"

I laughed along with the lady, because she seemed so pleased with herself, but I really couldn't see the point of her joke. She must have sensed my bewilderment because she added, "How many people who are 83 still have their own teeth?"

It was one of those moments when the future revealed itself, loud and clear. This very rich lady was not impressed with her Rolls Royce, with her designer dress, with living in fabled Santa Barbara. But owning gums as good as her gems was a source of inordinate pride. She was impressed with herself for having invested the time and bucks to maintain the set of teeth that she came equipped with over four score years ago.

I thought about my own children's attitudes toward investment. Their generation enjoys dealing in futures. They are into body building, cycling, jogging, triathlons and nutrition. But they may yet live to realize that "No Pain No Gain" pertains to their mouths as well as their biceps. Flossing is only the first baby step toward healthy gums. Will the generation that was orthodonted before 20, that flossed before 30, respond to the call for better oral health?

As their beautiful bites approach middle age, and the dentist breaks the bad news that healthy gums will cost about the same as a new Buick — as well as involve pain and swelling — a generation that grew up with the Beatles and Timothy O'Leary will simply respond, "Pass the Laughing Gas."

Famous cat lies

L ie Number One: The time is five o'clock.
   As per our pre-nuptial agreement, my husband feeds the cats and I feed the dog. That way we receive equal opportunity adoration. At precisely five o'clock the dog arrives in the kitchen, starts butting her head against my knees, then stares imploringly and maybe drools a bit. Not subtle, but effective.

   Theoretically, the cats get fed at five, too. By three o'clock they start following my husband, hurling their little bodies in front of him, jumping into his lap and mewing pitiful little kibble wails. Perhaps my husband's heart is softer than mine because the cats are frequently able to convince him that three o'clock is five. Call it Catlight Savings Time.

   Lie Number Two: What broken vase on the floor?
   I came home from an afternoon of shopping. There, in the middle of the living room floor were shards of a broken vase surrounded by daisy petals and water puddles. Turning to our animals I said in a stern voice, "Who did this?" My dog Jammer's tail sank beneath her legs; her head dipped to the floor and by her hang-dog look, she confessed to a crime she did not commit. Dogs are big on confessing.

   When I turned to the cats and said in a sterner voice, "Who did this?" they each opened one eye and regarded me with total boredom. Brazenly, they stepped around the clutter, yawned and looked at me as though to say: "You slattern. What's taking you so long to clean up this mess?"

Lie Number Three: That's not my dead lizard.

Around a ranch, we would prefer killer cats to help keep gophers and mice under control. Our tiger-striped cats are fairly business-like and merciless, but fat, fluffy Delilah is averse to killing anything that has hair on it. She prefers to slaughter careless butterflies and slow lizards. She carries her prey into our back room, drops them into a steep-sided laundry tub and watches as they try to escape — as though they were prime zoo specimens. Anybody who says that man is the only animal who kills for sport has never owned a cat.

Cat Lie Number Four: If you let me sleep on your bed, I'll stay down by your feet.

The goal of all domestic pets is to stake out the exact geographical center of your bed and claim it as their very own. They don't care if you must curl your body into a pretzel then toss and turn all night — just as long as you don't disturb them. Consequently, we force our menagerie to sleep in the laundry room. Delilah isn't very bright, but she does have one trick. She can open doors. If we don't push the door until we hear the latch click, she will wait until the middle of the night, hook her little claw under the door, then pick at it until it pops open.

At that point all the animals pad through the house and into the bedroom. The dog is always a bit hesitant about how she will be received at 3 a.m. but the cats are blatant. They demand our pillows, insist that we lift the covers so they can crawl under them.

The Biggest Cat Lie of All Time: I haven't slept a wink all day.

Mother's Day is for miracles

Every Mother's Day, now that my children are grown, I always give thanks for two things: I didn't kill them — and they didn't kill me.

I was a fairly typical first-time mother, back then in the '50s. In my fourth year of college I suddenly became aware that my degree would read — ironically — Bachelor of Arts. Or worse, Old Maid of Arts. In the opinion of most people a woman's primary reason for going to college was to catch a man.

Big deal! I went out and caught one.

What I hadn't anticipated was getting pregnant a couple of months later. Still, it was all a great adventure. I figured that a wedding, a college degree and a baby within twelve months was an economical use of my time. Motherhood sounded so exciting! After all those years in college, how tough could it be to do something women had been doing forever? I read up on it, like I was studying for an exam.

My first-born's was the first diaper I had ever changed, the first burp I had ever summoned. Oh, but Keith cried! And cried. And cried.

So did I.

I felt like I had been yanked out of the security of warm library stacks and thrown under a cold shower. One winter day, when I hadn't been out of the house for over a week and hadn't slept much, I did something I still regret. I spanked that little baby. Hard. Too hard.

Fortunately his father stepped in. He insisted that I go visit a good friend, a lady who was a veteran of the baby wars; she dispensed coffee and understanding. It never happened again, although many times I was tempted to hurt first and think later. Maybe it's a miracle that we don't read about a lot more cases of mothers killing their children.

We had two more children, a total of three within two and a half years. Strong patience was forged day by day as I got better at the business of mothering — involving, as it does, more art than science. And I liked it.

A few years later we all underwent a divorce. It isn't ever just parents who get divorced. Children get divorced, too. But somehow we coped and there were good times. I liked talking to kids, exploring the world with them, finding out what they thought, sharing a giggle. Not that I did everything right. Nobody does. But things didn't go too badly until . . .

Suddenly those cute little kids were as big as I was and getting bigger as all three slammed into their teens. Those are the years when kids cut their parents loose, not the other way round. In the process of weaning me, things got very tense. Adolescent hormones broke on the shores of parental authority. Raging storms and emotional turmoil became our norm.

Fortunately, crises usually happened one kid at a time, whether it was staying out too late, trouble at school or experimenting with drugs. I just tried to deal with each emergency as it arose. Had all three kids ever turned on me at once — they were big enough to kill me and frequently they were angry enough. News stories about kids who kill their parents are even rarer than ones exposing child abuse!

These days my children and I sometimes talk about things that happened while they were growing up. One day I summoned up courage and apologized to my oldest son for hitting him. Keith reacted to my tears with amusement. "Forget it Mom," he said, "I did."

Every year on Mother's Day I think about our miracle — we didn't kill each other.

Cranky for coffee

I've been addicted to a Columbian substance for 35 years. It is known by a lot of street names: mocha, java, mud, leaded, jolt. I refuse to acknowledge any government study or health expert who tries to come between me and my fix.

How severely addicted I am to coffee became very clear not too long ago. Because we were to have blood drawn early in the day for a cholesterol test, my beloved and I bravely fasted through the waking-up experience without so much as a rousing cup of buzz.

By 9:30 a.m. when our friendly, neighborhood vampire finally sucked blood into her enormous syringes, we were two cranky people headed for Carrows. For the first time in our marriage, we almost yanked the license plates from the bumpers of the car and sliced each other to ribbons right there in front of the clinic. For a fleeting second, I wished I were single again.

At the crowded restaurant, we were given the option to wait 10 minutes for a booth or to be seated immediately at the counter. No choice there, we quickly folded our fannies onto stools. With hands raised in supplication, we hailed the waitress. Do those wonderful women understand their power? At that moment we would have given her the deed to the ranch in exchange for a cup of coffee.

As that plump angel rotated her wrist, the sound of fresh coffee lapping into the cup was sweeter than rain on the roof after a long drought. We twirled the dark brown stuff over our tongues with the joy of wine connoisseurs discovering an ancient burgundy.

After just half a cup, my husband's basic chemistry began to reverse as the wrinkles on his face smoothed out. Before my very eyes he turned from Mr. Hyde back to Dr. Jekyll. My Dorian Gray's face lost 10 years! And he smiled, and squeezed my hand.

The mere suggestion of coffee will occasionally revive me. Sometimes, if I am in a big hurry and if it's been too long between cups, I stick my head into Starbucks and inhale deeply. What a clean, cheerful place to get a fix! Or if I'm in Lucky's I sidle up to those bags of beans in those little belch bags and surreptitiously squeeze one or two, just to shove some essence up my nose.

But I'm beginning to worry about where my future fixes are coming from. Has my favorite Columbian, Juan Valdez, quit picking beans and gone over to cultivating cocaine? I'm worried sick that Juan and his burro will get mixed up with those swarthy guys who pack automatic guns and spray bullets around with all the abandon of a housewife deodorizing her cat box.

Is anybody in Columbia left to pick the coffee? For years, I've sort of looked to Juan Valdez as my friend in the coffee business. I realize that times have been harder for Juan lately, what with trying to figure out which bushes have decaffeinated beans on them. I suppose in the off season he helps graft almond, chocolate and amaretto buds onto their limbs.

If Juan ever decides to take off his serape and quit picking coffee, there won't be any choice but to land the Marines. Next to oil, this country runs on coffee!

Will Cinderella get to the mall?

When it comes to shopping, my husband's idea of patience is the 15 minutes between the time he sets the brake and says, "Got everything you need?"

My daughter Drew, upon learning I had never visited an outlet mall, took pity on me. We drove south from Phoenix toward a place called Casa Grande. At the sight of brand names like Liz Claiborne the two of us leapt from the car and swam through four hours of the female equivalent of a feeding frenzy. We tore through shops, fingered our way through sleeves in search of price tags and swallowed up bargains. Around us swarmed schools of other women who were doing exactly the same thing. Most of them were — mature. In fact, the mall looked as though Sun City had opened its gates and disgorged its entire contents.

It took me an hour or so to realize that a large percentage of the people at the mall were not sharing our enthusiasm. It seems that the female half of a retired couple does pretty much what she's always done. She shops. The male half? Well, he drives her to the mall. Once there, he plops down and tries to keep out of his wife's hair.

I noted a fellow sitting off to one corner behind a rack of women's suits. He wore a windbreaker; atop his head was a cap that said "John Deere." If you could die of boredom, the guy looked terminal. In fact, no mortician would offer a corpse for viewing with such a sour look on his face. Stuck there, if he had died it might have been half an hour before his wife noticed anything was wrong.

"Not much to interest you here, huh?" I offered.

"I'll say."

"They should give you some magazines to read while you're sitting."

"Lots of stores don't even give you chairs."

Suddenly I realized that most stores and malls could be accused of gender abuse. Even at a convenient local mall, after my husband has lavished 12 minutes on the buying of a shirt, what's left for him? Nothing. Even the windows in Victoria's Secret rate no more than a passing glance when he races toward the parking lot.

How about a "men's only room" where they can read magazines about cars, guns, boats, trains, fishing — even girls. Hey, they could have a deck of cards. Why not add a screening room? VCRs could replay championship sports (including the best tackles) car races (including the best crashes) or decisive battles of World War II (including planes, ships and tanks blowing up.) There's always C-SPAN and bass fishing derbies.

Some malls offer babysitting. But has anybody ever done a time/income study, to determine how much more money grandma will spend if her husband is occupied? Many times I have fled after a single purchase because my husband starts weaving from one foot to another like a tall tree twisting in the wind. And just when the price tags are starting to bite.

"You know the best part of this?" my daughter asked as we drove back to Phoenix.

"What Drew?"

"We didn't take our husbands."

Surviving your pet

The other night I stumbled over Delilah, our dark gray stealth cat, on my way to the bathroom. She takes advantage of shadows, nights and closets to lurk. Dark places are her camouflage. Headlong I fell, bumping my head on a door jamb. The cat let out a yowl of surprise loud enough to alert neighbors to call the SPCA. I had no injury more serious than a bump on my head. Delilah escaped — nay bolted — with harm to her dignity but not to her paws.

I got to wondering. How many people are endangered, killed or maimed by their pets? Often, we hear heroic stories about people who risked life and limb to save dogs and cats caught in disasters. During one flood, a TV news helicopter picked up a stranded man, along with his dog, and ferried both to safety. I've been in helicopters a couple of times; they are fragile little things. If I were the pilot of such an expensive aircraft, I couldn't view rescuing a homeless person and his big muddy dog from an island on a flooded riverbed with much enthusiasm. The pilot reported that the dog was calm and didn't attempt to take over the piloting chores. I'm not sure my dog would have behaved as well. At a bare minimum, the wagging of her tail would probably have grounded the aircraft.

Many years ago my brother Dwight had a wonderful dog named Jeep. Jeep was advertised as a cocker spaniel, but his mother must have entertained strangers in the night. Jeep looked like a small black labrador retriever. Obedient, trainable, he also had a good sense of humor.

One June day while Dwight was trout fishing, his dog fell into a swollen mountain stream and got caught in the current. Jeep was trapped in an eddy next to the steep bank and although the animal struggled and struggled, he couldn't scramble to dry land. His nose was barely above water and it seemed he was about to dog-paddle his last stroke.

My brother jumped into the icy water, then boosted the dog to the bank. Only then did Dwight realize that he himself was in trouble, quickly losing his body heat to hypothermia in water which had been snow half an hour earlier. Finally, Dwight managed to hoist himself out of the swift, frigid river. Gleeful, the dog jumped all over Dwight and licked his face.

To the wonder of those watching, the faithful master started screaming obscenities at his dog. Wrapped in a blanket, Dwight explained through the chatting of his teeth, "Jeep licked my face and it made me mad." My brother had nearly lost his life saving the dog.

Every winter we read about Minnesotans or Michiganders who lose their lives while attempting to rescue a dog that has fallen through thin ice. But except for a vicious pit bull or rottweiler, headlines rarely read: "Dog kills man." You can attack motherhood and apple pie, but we cherish the legacy that pets save lives. Stories that make the news are about parrots who scream in the night to alert a family that their house is burning down, about dogs who stay by babies in blizzards, about cats who frighten away burglars by yowling.

Does anybody keep statistics on how many little old ladies get tripped up by their poodles and break their hips? How many cats knock flower pots off balconies, smashing the heads of people below? How many people chase parakeets into traffic?

Some statistics are better not kept. If publicity ever puts pets on the endangered species list, I'll never read another newspaper.

Sticking together through the night

It was like a bad dream, but I was wide awake. Immobilized in my own warm, cozy bed, I could not move my arms, my legs. I could not turn over. The clock radio gleamed forth 11:58. For more than an hour I had worked, without success, at the task of getting to sleep.

Finally it dawned on me. Once again, I was the victim of a trend.

Like most of us, I pride myself on staying serenely above trends. Somehow I hadn't thought of flannel sheets as trendy. For months all those catalogs depicted warm, cozy people in front of their warm, cozy fireplaces getting ready to settle into their warm, cozy flannel sheets for a warm, cozy sleep. And of course they wore warm, cozy flannel night shirts.

I fell for the Eddie Bauer look — hook, line and sinker.

What I hadn't figured on is that when you wear a flannel nighty and slip between flannel sheets the end effect is something like bedding down in Velcro armor. You're stuck there.

Fighting for sleep, my bedtime history passed before my eyes.

Even today, I can smell the oily tent-canvas I slept under when I was a little child camping with my family. Every evening, my daddy would heat rocks in the campfire, wrap them in newspaper and tuck mine into my sleeping bag. Every member of the family got one.

I confess that in the 1970s I warmed myself beneath an electric blanket. At the time, I thought mine was pretty nifty. That was before the media blasted forth warnings that electric blankets can kill, maim and sterilize.

One terrible night, at my little house high in the mountains of Colorado, the temperature plummeted 20 degrees below zero outside. Sometime in the middle of the night, the electricity went off. I awoke shivering, to a frigid house. It took me quite a while to figure out that my electric blanket had turned on me. I cursed at it for sucking my body heat back through the wires.

Wear socks to bed? There's something so tacky about wearing socks to bed. My mother was too prim to advise me to never go to bed with a man wearing his socks. I learned that myself — and passed it on to my daughter. He's not there for the long haul.

One evening over dinner my husband and I were reminiscing about visits we made to England — separately — back in the 1950s. I remembered gracious bed and breakfast hosts who offered a hot water bottle to take the chill off the sheets. How comforting that was.

Hey, why not try it? Along with flannel sheets, a hot water bottle offers a cheap, low-tech solution to cold feet. And you can blame it if you hear friendly little gurgles in the middle of the night.

I absolutely refuse to return to another trend — cold satin sheets. However, if I can just find a nice slippery satin nightshirt in Victoria's Secret catalog things might heat up nicely.

From guacamole to eternity

Years before he planned to retire from the aerospace industry, my husband figured out how he would spend his time. He planted and tended avocado trees here on his acres in Carpinteria. His idea was to provide the corn chips of our nation with great vats of guacamole to dip themselves in.

Unfortunately, the trees were ravaged by fungus, a drought sent the price of water to irrigate them soaring, a freeze denuded the leaves and every year, the price of fruit sagged. What a shame! A long, tall guy like Don — who doesn't need a ladder to prune and pick — belongs in an orchard.

He had lavished too much work, water and fertilizer on his trees to simply cut them down and burn them as firewood. He threatened to write a book entitled: *101 Ways to Lose Money on Avocados.* It was discouraging to watch the leather-green leaves drop to the ground. Bare limbs and stumps marched up and down our hillside.

One day, when I walked into the garage he had a wild look in his eye and brandished an ax. He sounded just like a mugger as he ordered me: "Put your arms up in the air. Reach! Higher! There." He then turned to attack a former tree trunk with his blade. He studied the way my back looked when I raised my arm, nodded, and gave me permission to leave.

Eventually, the torso of a long, lean, Modigliani-type

nude emerged from the tree trunk. He dubbed her "Venus de Avocado." He was delighted with the results. He says he found the wood to be soft enough to carve easily, yet its finished surface resembled hardwood. He explained that it didn't have many knots and its honest grain led him to carve along interesting contours. A variety of birds, animals, human torsos, musical instruments — even an abstract totem pole — took new life from the dead trees.

In his former life, when he worked as a mechanical engineer, he designed latches and rotary actuators for the space shuttle; he also planned machinery that moved luggage into the holds of airliners. He utilized that talent for visualizing three-dimensional concepts when he designed his sculptures. His mechanical ability also came in handy when it became necessary to move ever larger tree trunks.

I thought to myself that our live trees must be alarmed by his beaverly preoccupation with sculpting. He might have scalped the hillside bare, but instead began working with pine, walnut, oak and various woods from other places.

But Donald wanted people to see his work. He held no illusions that some gallery owner would beat a path to our ranch. First he hit upon the idea of putting his musical pieces in the window of a vacant store in a nearby shopping center. Eventually he joined various art associations and guilds so he could enter pieces in more traditional shows around Santa Barbara.

Inevitably, when someone looks at one of his silky nude forms, I am asked, "Are you the model?"

To which I reply, "Well, parts of me are."

Flat-chested at the prom

My plump little mother said, "You will not wear a strapless dress to the prom." In Mother's mind there would be two kinds of girls going to the prom at Wichita High School North in the spring of 1954: ones who wore strapless dresses and went all the way, as opposed to "good girls" like me who wouldn't dream of doing either.

Actually, I did dream of going all the way, but I knew I wouldn't because if I did, my date would be sure to figure out my deepest, darkest secret. *I wore falsies.* I couldn't handle the humiliation if he found out. I dreamed of a strapless dress, too, but with nothing to hold it up, it probably would have ended up down around my knees.

My role models were Jane Russell and Marilyn Monroe. After years of glancing down my shirt front, hoping to see some "development," my mother and I had decided a padded bra was the answer to the problem. But it didn't help much because I habitually hunched my shoulders in the hope that nobody would notice my chest.

Sex was a deep, dark secret in that "pre-pill era." We had no AIDs, no herpes — although we had heard a little bit about syphilis and gonorrhea. Yet we were very, very careful about sex because getting pregnant was a real, all-too-frequent possibility. No young person today can possibly understand the humiliation a woman suffered if it was whispered: "She had to get married." But it wasn't fear of venereal disease or pregnancy that kept me virtuous.

Nope, I was in terror of having a guy find out I wore falsies.

"Girls get the worst of this prom business, what with needing an expensive dress and all," said Mother. In those days, all a boy needed was a suit, a corsage and the keys to his father's car. A banquet would be held in the school cafeteria followed by a dance in the gym. Hotels had beds and the Elks Club were known to be bastions of sin, consequently both were off limits for such parties.

Although my mother complained about the dress, I believe she was more thrilled than I was when I told her that a tall guy in my English Lit class had invited me to the prom. She would get to make a dress! I never learned to sew, perhaps because I am left handed, which confused my mother more than it did me. Besides, sewing was her favorite recreation. Mother could spend hours flipping through pattern books, marveling at this gore or that gusset. She would not climb down from her stool until droplets of mist from my yawns threatened to sprinkle Mr. McCall's slick pages. One of the few times Mother behaved in an overtly sensuous manner was when she started feeling up fabric. She never left the store until every bit of stuff had passed between her thumb and fingers. She settled on something pink, nylon and netty.

After the actual construction began, Mother complained she had to "chase me down and hog-tie me" for fittings. I dreaded it when she said, "That doesn't hang just right," because I knew I would be required to turn around and around until everything was pinned to her satisfaction or I fainted from dizziness, whichever came first.

One day when I came home from school Mother

called down the stairs: "I figured it out!"

What she had figured out was to plant my falsies right into the bodice of the dress. There on the hanger was my dress — finished and pressed. All it needed was a head. Mine. The figure was already there.

The big night finally arrived. "Nice dress," said my escort, as he pinned on my carnations.

Mother beamed.

When my date and I "parked" after the prom, I tried to limit his explorations to areas above the neck. But never shall I forget the moment when he thrust his hand down the front of my dress and realized that he had just parted my body from its breasts. Poor guy, for a moment he wore this look of terror in the moonlight; he must have thought he had just delaminated me. I can still hear his embarrassed laughter after all these years. My face reddens to think of my humiliation.

I could hardly wait to graduate and get out of Wichita.

How to empty the nest

Once upon a time, so the story goes, children went off into the world forever — leaving their lonely, grieving parents knocking about in a big empty house. Psychologists even had a name for it: Empty-Nest Syndrome. That happy myth has vanished into the mists of time.

Perhaps I should explain that my children were aged eight, nine and ten at the time of my divorce. As custodial parent, I resigned myself to shelving my own social life, figuring it would be easier to grit it out and fly solo through their teenage years. Besides, I'd be skeptical about the sanity of any man who was crazy enough to want to marry a woman with three teenaged children. "When they reach 18, I told myself, they'll leave and I'll still be a young woman." I had a few things in mind to do with the rest of my life — after we all grew up.

Although I warned the children about how tough life really is, they were determined to leave. Each, in turn, said something to the effect: "I'm sick of this dump. I'm going to get my own place to live and a good job." They packed a suitcase or back pack and tooled off down the road. One son paused just long enough to letter a sign that read: ANYWHERE BUT HERE. He said it got him a lot of rides. One took off on a bicycle. A third chugged off down the road in a puff of smoke, emitted from the tailpipe of a terminal Kharmann Ghia.

I barely got used to finding the tub clean every time I wanted a soak when, abruptly, each came back — with flattering things to say about home. "Boy were you ever smart, Mom. It's a tough cruel world out there. What's for dinner?"

After the temporary euphoria of feeling my warnings were validated, it slowly sank in. They had no intention of leaving, at least not in the near future. They intended to stay with me until fame, fortune and easy bucks came knocking on our door — preferably with an engraved invitation and a lifetime guarantee.

This Return-to-the-Nest Syndrome is particularly serious when parents happen to live near a ski area or the beach. In my case, it was a ski area. When these fully grown birds flew back, the nest seemed even smaller, messier and noisier than it had been before. I began to plot how to push those chicks out of the nest, even though their claws were clinging on for dear life. I tried a lot of things. I cooked not, neither did I clean. I collected rent. At night I slept with my car keys on a string around my neck.

There was one memorable evening when I was at the home of a friend — a special male friend. We were preparing a candlelight dinner for two. My eldest son phoned. "Hi mom. What's for dinner?"

"Whatever you want to fix," I replied.

"Aren't you coming home?" He sounded surprised.

"No. Make something for yourself."

There was a pause at the other end of the phone then his voice arose with indignation. "Mother!" he exclaimed. "This food is all frozen."

Something cracked. At that moment I realized motherly virtues would never get my children — or me —

to a state of self-sufficiency. I pondered. I plotted. Finally, I resolved upon a campaign of action. The strategy? I called it Scorched Earth Refrigerator.

After a couple of weeks our larder reached an alarming state of empty. The children looked worried, but nobody offered to buy groceries. The only thing left in the cupboard was a couple of boxes of a well-known prepared macaroni and cheese product that the kids always called Crap Dinner. My ploy helped, temporarily. Eventually, I did find a solution, although it might not work for everybody.

I ran away from home and got married.

You only die once

Almost any Saturday morning, little signs on neighborhood telephone poles serve as treasure maps, luring me to seek my fortune. The itch to hit the garage sale circuit must be scratched.

There is a hierarchy of garage sales. Hastily scribbled signs that announce lawn sales, carport sales or yard sales are the lowliest. I feel a little uneasy at some garage sales because I have the feeling that the sellers are pulling junk out of their closets, trying to raise enough dough to cover their next mortgage payment. When I look around, I wonder if some sleazy looking buyers may take advantage of the occasion to case the joint.

Moving sales are better, although the merchandise often seems to consist of what wouldn't fit in the moving van. Maybe sellers hope people will buy what's left so they won't have to pay to have it hauled to the dump.

Divorce sales are very strange. Am I buying the one thing that caused the couple to split up? Would it be bad luck to take home that lampshade shaped like the Liberty Bell?

There's a wonderful anonymity about swap meets. I frequently attend the monthly swap meet at our local historical museum. I'm fascinated by the lady who dresses up like a clown to sell wristwatches, by the woman who crochets with such ferocious intensity that she has no time to bother making a sale, by the guy who rescues old appliances and makes them useful again. In every treasure hunter's heart lurks the certainty that out there somewhere is a seller who cannot read well enough to decipher the word Spode on the reverse of a platter

But the creme-de-la-creme of off-road shopping is a good estate sale. To me, estate sales are the equivalent of hunting for treasure in the Caribbean. I'm convinced I will turn up a hoard that time forgot. I'm so excited I don't even complain about waiting in line for an hour before the doors open because I can hardly wait for the grabbing to start. Will there be china? Silver? Linen? Even if I don't buy anything, sometimes an estate sale is a good chance to glimpse the lifestyles of the previously rich and famous.

But even in the presence of magnificent antiques, I'm edgy at estate sales, too. In the back of my mind I can see gangs of rapacious buyers rummaging through my precious things, snickering about what kind of a weirdo would own a "foot stool" with sneakers on its legs.

Oh well, you only die once.

One Saturday morning I received a flash of insight about the meaning of life here in the Santa Barbara area. You keep going to estate sales, acquiring antiques and used stuff, upgrading your household goods — until it's your turn.

Chia Pet sprouts memories of grandma

Sometimes I like to think ahead clear into the next century — to imagine how my grandchildren will think of me as I was at Christmas time, a way back in the 1900s.

There are the kiddies, gathered in my attic. Oops! I don't have an attic. So maybe they will be going through my things in my mini-storage. Lots of grannies are getting their own mini-storage units these days. Some are grateful that they don't have to live in them. Who knows whether 21st Century children will be hippies, punks or zoot suiters? Teenagers don't change, they just look progressively weirder. But please children, no safety pins in your ears or pierced noses. Have a little respect for my memory!

I can see little Angela picking up a pottery specimen, slightly chipped. Maybe one of its peggy legs is missing. Even so, she will know that it was once a small goat with a green face. As tears fill her eyes she will say: "This was grandma's Chia Pet. Remember when we gave her the Chia Pet? We bought it for her down at the old Thrifty Drugstore. I used to love Thrifty Drug, that quaint little store at the mall where you could get a Hershey bar for 65 cents. It's part of Club Drug now."

"Sure," said Daniel. "Grandma used to smear seeds on it, water it and watch the little seeds sprout. But she'd get so sad when they all shriveled up and died. Grandma hated shrivel."

"Yes," said Naomi. "I remember. She tried and tried but her Chia Pet was never hairy enough to suit her."

"Grandma sure was great, though. Remember that Clapper that we gave her for Christmas?" said Ian. "Every time we came in the house she used to show us how it worked. She used to sit on the couch and clap the Christmas tree on and off so fast it just winked at you. She said it made her happy, reminded her of Las Vegas."

Liliana smiled sweetly as she remembered: "After Christmas she used to hook her Clapper up to the blender so she could sit in her rocking chair and clap up a margarita any time she got thirsty."

"But remember Christmas dinner?" said Natasha "That was the best part. Grandma would light the candles, put the turkey on the table, turn the lights down really low, then go from plate to plate with her Salad Shooter. She got so she could stand back five feet from the table and hit a plate with the cucumbers. When her batteries were fresh, nobody could shoot a salad like Grandma."

"I remember, all right." said Ariel "But I used to get really mad when she made such a big production of shooting radishes. Remember how we all hated radishes? When her eyesight got worse and her aim was off some radish slivers would end up floating in the gravy."

As they looked over Grandma's things their eyes grew misty.

"What ever happened to Grandma?" asked Daniel. "I haven't seen her for ages and I miss her so much."

Rose cleared her throat. As the oldest, she knew a few of the family's deepest, darkest secrets. "She ran off to Bora Bora with that telephone solicitor who called her up to tell her she had won a trip.

"She sold him on the idea of going with her and that was the last we saw of her. Isn't that just like Grandma? Stiffing us so we have to pay the rent on her mini-storage?"

Signs around the world

More books by Virginia Cornell available from Manifest Publications

Doc Susie: The True Story of a Country Physician in the Colorado Rockies

Winner: Two Benjamin Franklin awards, Publishers Marketing Association, 1991

> She was beautiful —
>> She was smart —
>>> She was dying

When Susan Anderson, M.D., stepped from the train into frigid Fraser, Colorado — "Icebox of the Nation" — she had everything to die for and nothing to live for. This is the true story of how Doc Susie recovered her health, then ventured forth on snowshoes, horseback or in cabooses to save the lives of lumberjacks, miners, ranchers, railroaders and their families. So desperate were they for medical attention that they didn't care that she was a *mere* woman. One woman's search for success and romance led her to a deeper love; her devotion to her working stiffs thrust her into confrontation with two of the most powerful men in the State. "Three years of research have contributed to a biography that reads like an adventure novel," Diane Donovan, *The Bookwatch*

Ski Lodge – Millers Idlewild Inn: Adventures in Snow Business

WINNER: Best Non-Fiction Book, National Federation of Press Women, Inc., 1993

High in the mountains, there was once a rustic, homemade ski lodge — populated by reluctant honeymooners, errant husbands, truant plumbers, youthful ski bums . . . plus one naive innkeeper. Virginia Cornell, the former innkeeper, invites you to check into the Miller family's funky old Inn high in the Rockies — where the grub was great and the powder was deep. With humor and insight the author remember when, as a single mother, she struggled to fill the gigantic footprints vacated by her frenetically energetic father. Her first year in the Inn business brought adventures — hilarious, romantic, tragic. Relive life as she skied it in the early 1970s. "A delightfully light-hearted account of innkeeping in the far simpler '70s," Joan Hinkemeyer, *Rocky Mountain News*

ORDER FORM

The following titles are available from Manifest Publications:
Indicate number of copies ordered:

☐ *The Latest Wrinkle and Other Signs of Aging* $10.95

☐ *Doc Susie: The True Story of a County
    Physician in the Colorado Rockies*   14.95

☐ *Ski Lodge: Adventures in Snow Business*   14.95

Shipping and handling per order
Book rate, U.S. Post Office   3.00

California residents add 7.75% tax   _____

Total Amount Enclosed   _____

Send to:

Name _____

Street Address or P.O. Box _____

City _____ State _____ Zip _____

Phone orders encouraged. (805) 684-4905

Or mail to:
Manifest Publications
P.O. Box 429
Carpinteria, CA 93014-0429